INITIAL
TEACHER
EDUCATION

INITIAL TEACHER EDUCATION

Policies and Progress

Edited by **Norman J Graves**

LONDON EDUCATION STUDIES

KOGAN PAGE Published in association with The Institute of
Education, University of London

First published in 1990 by Kogan Page Ltd,
120 Pentonville Road, London N1 9JN

Typeset at Selectmove Ltd, London
Printed and bound in Great Britain by Biddles Ltd, Guildford

British Library Cataloguing in Publication Data
A CIP record for this book is available from the British Library

ISBN 0–7494–0095–1

Contents

Notes on Contributors

Dr Richard Aldrich is Senior Lecturer in Education at the Institute of Education, University of London. He is a historian of education and has published *An Introduction to the History of Education* (Hodder & Stoughton) as well as numerous articles on the history of education.

Michael Naish is Senior Tutor for Initial Courses of Training at the Institute of Education. He is a geographer, one-time director of the Geography 16–19 Curriculum Development Project, co-author of the handbook on the project, as well as the author of textbooks and many articles on geographical education.

Dr Robert Cowen is Senior Lecturer in Comparative Education and Chairperson of the Department of International and Comparative Education at the Institute of Education. He is author of articles on the methodology of comparative education and editor (with P Stokes) of *Methodological Issues in Comparative Education* (London Association of Comparative Educationists).

Professor Norman Graves is Pro-Director (Professional Studies) at the Institute of Education. Originally a specialist in geographical education, he has written books in this field such as *Geography in Education* (Heinemann). His concern about education generally is reflected in his *The Education Crisis: Which Way Now?* (Christopher Helm).

Dr Dennis O'Keeffe is Senior Lecturer at the Polytechnic of North London in the Department of Teaching Studies. He is an expert in teacher education and has written many books, including (with Patricia Stoll) *Officially Present* (Institute of Economic Affairs).

Professor Keith Swanwick is Professor of Music Education and Chairperson of the Music Department at the Institute of Education. He is a well-known expert in music education, his latest book being *Music, Mind and Education* (Routledge). He has recently researched the views of students and teachers on teacher education.

Professor Sir William Taylor is Vice-Chancellor of the University of Hull and Chairman of the Council for the Accreditation of Teacher Education (CATE). He is a former Director of the Institute of Education. He has written many books on teacher education and edited *Metaphors of Education* (Heinemann).

Professor Alec Ross is Academic Secretary of the Universities Council for the Education of Teachers (UCET) and was formerly head of the School of Education at the University of Lancaster. He is also a former Chairman of UCET.

Professor Denis Lawton was Director of the Institute of Education until September 1989. He is an expert in the field of curriculum studies and has written a large number of books in the field of education, such as *The Politics of the School Curriculum* (Routledge).

Introduction

Norman Graves

In the last ten years there has been a spate of books and papers on professional education in general and on teacher education in particular. Given the current tendency in the United Kingdom for teacher training to be the object of scrutiny and reform by the government, the Publications Committee of the Institute of Education at the University of London thought it apposite that a collection of original papers be published on this important matter. I was given the task of editing this collection, as well as the freedom to choose my collaborators. I ought, therefore, to make clear the rationale for the structure of this book, and for the contributions it contains.

Perhaps it is important to explain at the outset that no attempt has been made to put over a particular line or policy about teacher education. Each author writes from his own point of view and experience, and it will be plain that they do not have a common stance. To cite only two examples, whilst Dennis O'Keeffe writes on the 'myths of teacher training', Keith Swanwick argues for the 'necessity of teacher education'. A second caveat is that whilst government publications in recent years have consistently used the term 'teacher training' rather than 'teacher education', in this book the two terms are used interchangeably, except where an author (for example Dennis O'Keeffe) makes a distinction. The terms are used to refer to the kinds of courses used to prepare students professionally for the teaching profession. We are writing, of course, about initial teacher education (ITE) in England and Wales, though reference may be made, from time to time, to in-service education and training (INSET).

It seemed to me important that the historical setting of ITE should be sketched out, so that we would be aware of the antecedents of our present system. Richard Aldrich has done this in the first chapter and shown how contextual factors in the economy and in political life have often influenced the nature and extent of teacher education. He has brought out parallels between the history of teacher education and its practice in the present day. Perhaps one of the most interesting parallels is that of apprenticeship, in view of the current government promotions of the Licensed and Articled Teacher Schemes. Although the parallel is not an exact one, it is worth noting that although pupil teachers were a cheap way of providing elementary education, they proved to be a much inferior product when compared with teachers coming out of training colleges. Eventually the pupil-teacher system disappeared. In bringing the story of teacher education to the present day, Richard Aldrich shows how the universities' involvement in the process stems to a large extent from the setting up of day training colleges. The universities were keen to develop educational studies in an academic sense and this led to the incorporation of educational theory into teacher-training courses. However, as more and more Postgraduate Certificate in Education (PGCE) students in higher education came to teach in primary and secondary comprehensive schools, so the emphasis on educational theory as a basis for practice began to be questioned.

In Chapter 2, Michael Naish outlines the nature of the present situation in teacher training, indicating the kind of developments which have taken place in the recent past. He describes the institutional bases in which teacher education is undertaken and shows why the PGCE route to becoming a teacher has become the dominant one. He contrasts the Bachelor of Education (BED) degree route to teaching with the PGCE and describes the essential structure of most teacher-training courses. In so doing he uses Bell's (1981) model of the changes which have occurred in courses since the 1950s. In order to provide a concrete present-day example of teacher education, he describes in some detail the PGCE course which he manages at the Institute of Education in London. However, this is seen as but one illustration of a general tendency in PGCE courses in the early 1990s.

The description given by Michael Naish provides a base from which to cast an eye over present and former practice overseas. It is salutary, as Robert Cowen indicates in Chapter 3, to note that other nations may not do things in the same way as we do, and indeed to note the mistakes which some have made in the past so as not to repeat them. I am sure that if we have not gone in for the extremes of competency-based teacher training, it is in part because we have learned from American experience. Cowen's illuminating approach is to ask two questions – Whom should the teachers serve? What should the teachers know? – and to give the answers which have been formulated in various parts of the world, but particularly in continental Europe and in North America. His analysis demonstrates that the teacher in training in England is at the receiving end of a number of messages as to whom he or she should serve, some of which are conflicting. Nevertheless, the trend seems clear: 'teachers are increasingly treated as employees, and as employees of large bureaucracies. Following management principles, they must possess measurable skills, have job descriptions, and be upgradable.' All this is in the context of schools seen as firms producing services for clients (the parents). The notion of the cultured teacher is disappearing.

In Chapter 4 I thought it important to analyse as closely as possible the ideas which influence current practice in teacher education and to trace their origin. Like medicine, education is an area prone to professional fashions, and if one is to distinguish between what is of value and what is factious, it is vital to scrutinize the intellectual validity of what is proposed as well as to evaluate its empirical workings. This is why I have spent some time outlining what seem to be the theoretical underpinnings to the current rhetoric of teacher education, based on Schön's notion of the 'reflective practitioner'. What makes Schön's ideas particularly valuable is that they were not developed in one professional context alone, but in a variety of professional contexts, and appear to have general rather than specific validity. Whilst the British empirical studies of the needs of teacher training were developed independently of Schön's work, nevertheless the relationship between them is not difficult to see. I attempt to synthesize the approaches to teacher education in a diagram which relates the various elements involved. One important aspect of creating the 'reflective practitioner', stressed by Schön, is that it takes time, something our 'masters' sometimes forget.

Dennis O'Keeffe, in Chapter 5, brings to teacher education a view usually associated with the radical right of politics. In essence he argues that while intellectual disciplines can be taught, teaching cannot: attempting to teach students how to teach is an impossible enterprise. Although this chapter may seem very different from the others, it is my view that the author is in accord with others in this volume in his belief that honest intellectual endeavour is what education is about. He argues that what is happening in teacher education is a manifestation of a much wider malaise in education generally: 'egalitarian, technicist and romantic ideologies' undermining essentially cultural and intellectual aims. He further argues that those engaged in the reform of teacher education have mistakenly perceived the problem as practical rather than intellectual. He can see no improvement occurring until what he calls the 'myths of teacher training' are abandoned.

In Chapter 6 on the other hand, Keith Swanwick maintains that his small-scale empirical investigation among PGCE students shows that these students would not have been happy simply to learn how to teach 'on the job'. He also argues, cogently, that schools at present have neither the time nor the resources to undertake the task of preparing future teachers for their professional careers.

The Chairman of the Council for the Accre
Education (CATE), Sir William Taylor, indic;
influenced teacher education since its incepti
interesting story he has to tell in Chapter 7,
that a body set up by the Secretary of State for F
to determine centrally, through its recommen
State, whether courses of teacher training sh
Clearly this chapter is written in a positive vein by
worked hard to ensure that CATE worked well. Not everyon
that CATE was necessity, though most will find it necessary to wo.
with it in order to get on with the job of teacher education. As Robert
Cowen has pointed out in Chapter 3, teachers are now enmeshed in a
much more bureaucratic situation than was the case ten years ago, and
CATE is one of the elements of this bureaucracy.

In Chapter 8, Alec Ross elaborates on the efforts made, so far
unsuccessfully, by the teaching profession, to set up a General Teaching
Council (GTC). The aim is to ensure that control of entry and entry
standards are guided, as in other professions, by a body representing
the profession itself. It is a long and fascinating story illustrating the
power struggle among the contestants. Clearly, such a body could not
coexist with CATE, and these two bodies can be considered rivals for
the function of controlling the standards of entry into the profession and
the nature of professional preparation.

Lastly, Denis Lawton, in looking at possible future scenarios, notes
that certain contradictions in policies (control of entry versus opening
up entry to teaching) will need to be resolved. He also sets teacher
education in the scene of the evolving education system, which he
believes may need to accept three grades of teachers: those who have
an initial qualification and can only undertake certain tasks; those who,
following a period of probation and further training, can undertake
a more extended professional role; and those who, having gained an
advanced professional qualification, obtain full professional status and
may carry out all the main tasks of a teacher including the supervision
of students. In such a system, initial training might be limited to
preparation for immediate classroom duties, leaving wider educational
issues for later courses.

No doubt the debate on ITE will continue. I hope that this book will
make a useful contribution to that debate.

Chapter 1

The Evolution of Teacher Education

Richard Aldrich

Introduction

This chapter is divided into four broad sections. The first three examine the origins of central elements in the evolution of teacher education: apprenticeship, training colleges and educational theory. In the final section, which addresses the question 'What is the best way, or what are the best ways, of educating teachers?', some historical and contemporary conclusions are drawn. The historian of education cannot provide conclusive answers as to how teachers should be educated in the present, or in the future, but it is possible to show how and why decisions about educating teachers were made in the past, and to make some assessment of the validity or otherwise of those decisions and of their outcomes.

This 'case-study' approach means that there is no intention to cover all the developments in the history of teacher education in this country; indeed, such a task would be manifestly impossible in a chapter of this length. Readers seeking such information might begin with Dent (1977) which provides an overview of the whole period from 1800 to 1975. Other general studies which have stood the test of time include those of Rich (1933, 1972) which covers the nineteenth century, and of Jones (1924) which provides a detailed picture, with historical introduction, of the early twentieth-century scene. Full details of these works, and of more specialist studies, are to be found in the list of references.

Two final points of introduction concern the title of this chapter. The term 'evolution' is not used to imply that there has been a long line of unbroken progress in teacher education. There is no assumption in respect of this subject, or indeed of any other, that a single historical thread leads to, and justifies, the present. The case-study method, indeed, is a deliberate attempt to avoid such a linear, and frequently celebratory, type of approach. In the various historical situations to be discussed below there were genuine alternative courses of action open, and choices to be made.

Nevertheless, over the last 150 years it has become widely, if not universally, accepted that those who are engaged in certain roles in society – for example doctors and dentists, priests and lawyers, drivers of heavy vehicles or railway trains, and pilots of aeroplanes – should have some initial formal training, and secure a licence or other form of certification, before they are allowed to perform these roles in an unsupervised way. The first government-sponsored teachers' certificate examinations in England took place in 1848, and it is a matter of fact that over the next 140 years teaching increasingly came to be, and to be seen to be, a job which necessitated some preliminary training and qualification. Indeed, by the 1980s new entrants amongst those who taught children in the compulsory years of formal schooling in the public sector were required to be both graduates and trained. This historical process may justifiably be described as a process of evolution.

The term 'teacher education' may be taken to subsume the concepts both of graduation or other educational qualification, and of training for teaching. The authors referred to above, Jones (1924), Rich (1933, 1972) and Dent (1977), all used the term 'teacher training' in the titles of their works. Books which concentrate upon more recent history, however, for example Lomax (1973) and Alexander, Craft and Lynch (1984), have been concerned with 'teacher education'. Such a change reflects in part the redesignation in the 1960s of the training colleges as colleges of education, institutions which, while producing teachers, were to engage in graduate-level studies, both in the area of education and in other subjects, although the final award was to be a Bachelor of Education degree. Nevertheless the term 'education' is to be preferred on other grounds. To be concerned solely with training is to run the risk of neglecting both a whole tradition of teacher preparation and a whole area of schools and schooling.

For much of English history the accepted method of preparation for holding the post of teacher or master in a grammar or public school, many private establishments, and indeed in the university itself, was a master's degree from the universities of Oxford or Cambridge. Such a qualification bore testimony to the recipient's competence in respect of the subject matter of study, rather than to his ability to impart that matter to others. (The term 'his' may be used in this context: until the second half of the nineteenth century women were rigorously excluded from these educational worlds both as teachers and students.) Even nineteenth-century pupil teachers and training-college students, moreover, spent much of their time in acquiring basic factual knowledge about the subject matter which they were to teach. The term 'teacher education' encompasses the issues of competence in subject matter and of the ability to impart it, and allows for a historical investigation of both these strands.

Apprenticeship

Examples of informal teacher apprenticeships can be found throughout English history. Teaching was frequently a family trade. In the first half of the nineteenth century, for example, both Rowland Hill, the inventor of the penny post, and Matthew Hill, the legal reformer, taught in their father's school at Hill Top, Birmingham.

In 1846, however, a formal system of pupil-teacher apprenticeship was established under the Minutes of the Committee of Council. Elementary-school pupils who were at least 13 years of age could be apprenticed to the school managers for a period of five years. They would teach in the school during the day and receive instruction from the master and mistress for a further one and a half hours. Apprentices were to be paid £10 a year, rising by annual increments to £20 a year. Teachers in charge of apprentices would receive £5 a year for one apprentice, £9 for two, and £3 for each subsequent one. Payments to apprentices and to teachers-in-charge depended upon a satisfactory report from the government inspector. Upon completion of their apprenticeships candidates could compete for 'Queen's Scholarships' of a further £20 or £25 per year which would enable them to proceed to training college, and so to achieve a teacher's certificate.

Not all pupil teachers went on to training college and to certification. For some the scheme was essentially a means of gaining further education for themselves, and of being paid for so doing. Others saw the apprenticeship as a qualification for occupations outside teaching; indeed, until 1852 apprenticeship as a pupil teacher was a recognized route into minor posts in the Civil Service. Others again proceeded directly into schools as teachers, though without certificated teacher status.

Judged in terms of numbers the pupil-teacher system was a success. In 1848 there were already some 2,000 in elementary schools in England and Wales, and by 1861, when the Newcastle Commission reported, 13,871 (Jones, 1924, p 190). A check was imposed by the Revised Code of 1862 which abolished the fixed rates of both pupil teachers' pay, and the augmentation of the salaries of those teachers who supervised and taught them, and led to a decline in overall numbers of some 5,000. Numbers of entrants, indeed, fell from 3,092 in 1862 to 1,895 in 1867. The rapid demand for teachers of all types consequent upon the Education Act of 1870, however, saw the Committee of Council imposing financial penalties on schools which did not employ specified numbers of pupil teachers, and over the next ten years figures more than doubled: from 14,612 to 32,128 (Dent, 1977, pp 25–6). The first decade of the twentieth century saw an even more dramatic decline in numbers. Though in 1900 there were still 30,783 pupil teachers – nearly one-quarter of the whole teaching force in elementary schools – by 1912–13 there were fewer than 2,000 (Dent, 1977, pp 47, 55).

Attitudes towards the apprenticeship method of training, as exemplified by the pupil-teacher system, have varied considerably. To some nineteenth-century contemporaries, including Matthew Arnold, they were the very 'sinews' of the elementary school. Others identified the pupil teachers as 'the weakest part of the system'. In their favour it can be stated with some certainty that pupil teachers were better than the monitorial system advocated by Lancaster and Bell. They were, moreover, a natural and widespread development and not simply created by government as the result of Kay-Shuttleworth's campaign, subsequent to his observation in 1838 of the running of a workhouse school by a 14-year-old monitor, William Rush, during the master's absence through illness.

Alexander (1978) has shown that in the 1830s 'pupil teachers' were being discussed by name, both in the quarterly press and in Select Committee. A pupil-teacher system had been in existence in Holland since 1816, and Cousin's report on Dutch education was available in English translation from 1838. Salary supplementation for teachers engaged in training pupil teachers also dates from the 1830s, and featured not only in Ireland and Scotland, but also in Lord John Russell's unsuccessful proposals of 1839 for teacher training in England and Wales. Finally, in this catalogue of antecedents to the 1846 Minutes, it should be noted that the London Diocesan Board launched a pupil-teacher scheme in 1844, and four years later provided a system of competitive scholarships to enable the best of those pupil teachers to proceed to St Mark's College.

There can be no doubt, moreover, that the pupil-teacher system served to supply the training colleges with a good supply of experienced and relatively mature recruits. Given that throughout the nineteenth century nearly all children left elementary school by the age of 12, and that training colleges recruited from the age of 18, the pupil-teacher system provided a most important bridge. It provided, indeed, a substitute secondary, or higher elementary, education for children who would have had no chance of access to grammar, public or equivalent private schools. No doubt many of those teachers who supervised the work of the pupil teachers, and instructed them after school hours, also benefited from the experience.

School managers, and central government itself, might also have good cause to welcome pupil teachers, for the simple reason that they were very cheap. A certificated master could cost as much to employ as eight young pupil teachers. Even in 1900 there was only one trained teacher per 128 pupils in elementary schools (Dent, 1977, p 51).

Nevertheless the weaknesses of the pupil-teacher system became increasingly apparent, and led to its abolition in the early years of the twentieth century.

Pupil teachers, on the whole, were not as good at teaching as 'proper' teachers. Their simple lack of years (in recognition of this fact in 1900 the minimum age for a pupil teacher was raised to 15 years and in 1904 to 16, though with exceptions), and inexperience in both learning and teaching, were considerable handicaps. Another difficulty was that many pupil teachers spent all their lives in an elementary-school environment, and thus were denied any real access to the type of education available to their social superiors. In 1907, in recognition of this problem, a bursary scheme was introduced to enable intending teachers to stay on at secondary schools, although such bursars could still spend a year as a student teacher in an elementary school before entering training college. The success of the scheme was such that within a matter of three years there were more bursars than pupil teachers in English schools.

Other, more fundamental, problems may also be laid at the door of – or at least associated with – apprenticeship teaching. In his comparative study of 'Western' nineteenth-century rural primary teachers, Lauglo (1982) highlighted the lowly status and social isolation of English elementary schoolteachers. The pupil-teacher system, which proclaimed that teaching a class of some 60 children was a task which could be entrusted to a teenaged apprentice, was a significant factor not only in depressing the status of teachers and teaching, but also of learners and learning. Parallel practices were not to be found in such professions as the Church, law and medicine. Pupil teachers reflected the low priority accorded by the governing classes in nineteenth-century England to the schooling of the poor. In many other countries teaching was a job for adults.

Training colleges

The first training colleges of modern times in England were those established in London at the start of the nineteenth century to train teachers in the monitorial system of teaching. At Borough Road, Southwark, and Baldwin's Gardens off the Gray's Inn Road, adult teachers, and intending teachers, came for short courses of instruction in the respective methods of Lancaster and Bell.

The decline of the monitorial system hastened the development of a broader type of teacher training, and the establishment of residential colleges. By 1860 there were 34 training colleges, a number which had grown to 43 by 1890 when the first day training colleges were established. Even in 1900, however, they were supplying only some 4,000 student places, while barely a quarter of the teaching force in elementary schools at that date was college-trained.

This situation reflected in large part the inability of the voluntary system to cope with the problem. Almost without exception nineteenth-century colleges were owned and run by the religious bodies, and after 1860 received no government grants for capital expenditure. In consequence, under the terms of the Education Act of 1902, suitably amplified by Board of Education Regulations in 1903 and 1904, the new local education authorities (LEAs) were empowered to assist the existing colleges and to establish their own. By 1970, when there were some 157 colleges of education in existence, the majority were LEA controlled.

Nineteenth-century school inspectors had no doubt as to the general superiority of trained teachers over the untrained. In 1861 the Report of the Newcastle Commission contained considerable evidence on this point. Thus HMI Brookfield, a man 'not at all disposed to overvalue the effects of training', reported that his inspection of some 470 schools conducted by trained teachers, and 215 by untrained, had yielded the results shown in Table 1.1.

	Good %	Fair %	Inferior %
Schools under trained teachers	24	49	27
Schools under untrained teachers	3	39	58

Figure 1.1 *Quality of schools under trained and untrained teachers, 1861*
Source: *Newcastle Commission Report*, 1861, vol 1, pp 149–50.

Three broad approaches to teacher training had emerged in the colleges by 1860. The first, that of pastoral simplicity, of service and humility, of character formation, and of a seminary mentality, may be associated with Battersea College, and with the aims and work of Kay-Shuttleworth. In 1839 he had inspected Vehrli's training school at Kreuzlingen, and had there been impressed by the commitment of the students, who wore wooden shoes and no stockings, rose at four in the morning, retired after a full day at nine in the evening, and were prepared for the rigours of life among peasants. In 1840 Kay-Shuttleworth, who had been pondering the problems of securing a supply of teachers for workhouse schools – a particularly grim, depressing and full time occupation – opened a private college at Battersea which he himself would superintend. Though financial problems soon forced Kay-Shuttleworth to hand the college over to the National Society, the basic features there established – the 'master of method', the 'model school', the inordinately long and meticulously timetabled day – became essential features of the training regime. Kay-Shuttleworth proclaimed that as a result of 'this laborious and frugal life . . . the master goes forth into the world humble, industrious and instructed' (Kay-Shuttleworth, 1862, pp 404–5). Rich (1972, p 75) described the experiment at Battersea as 'the most significant event in the history of the development of the English training college.'

St Mark's College, Chelsea, another National Society College, founded in 1841, provided a vision of both teachers and their training totally at variance with that of Battersea. Its first principal, Derwent Coleridge, the second son of the poet and philosopher Samuel Taylor Coleridge, was a graduate of St John's College, Cambridge. Derwent Coleridge, who for 14 years had been master of the grammar school at Helston in Cornwall, was a renowned scholar, possibly the most accomplished linguist of his day. In addition to his proficiency in the classical and modern European languages, Coleridge could read Arabic, Coptic and Zulu. He was quite prepared to recruit boys from grammar schools into St Mark's, and to enable his charges to engage in some upward social mobility. In the first two years of their three-year course students were concerned solely with their own education. Latin was the principal subject of study, and much emphasis was also placed upon worship in the college chapel. Such worship, which was characterized by elaborate sung services, helped to fuel the criticism that St Mark's students were better qualified to become Anglo-Catholic priests than to be teachers of the humble poor.

Coleridge retired in 1864. Under his guidance St Mark's was providing an important alternative model for teacher training. In part it exemplified the ideas of those who looked back to the revival of the bishop's licence for teaching, and to the concept of schoolmaster-deacons. It also encompassed the ideal of preparation for teaching in a range of schools. In 1864, indeed, less than half of those trained at St Mark's were working in inspected schools. Some had entered the Church.

Though the traditions of St Mark's, and of its sister college, Whitelands, were to survive in modified form into the twentieth century, the revisions of the training college syllabus and examinations carried out in the 1850s by HMIs Moseley and Cook, coupled with the payment-by-results era introduced by the Revised Code in 1862, ensured the victory of the Battersea approach.

That victory was also won at the expense of a third model, exemplified by Chester College and its first principal, Arthur Rigg. The college, opened in 1840, was the product of the Chester Diocesan Board, itself established in the previous year. Its founders included John Sumner, the future Archbishop of Canterbury, Edward Stanley, who was to be a Conservative prime minister on three occasions, and William Gladstone, who was to be a Liberal prime minister on four. The foundation was a multi-purpose one. In addition to the training college with places for 50 residential students, there was a middle-class boarding school for 70 pupils, and an elementary day school for 110 pupils. This last would serve as a practising school (Bradbury, 1975).

Rigg, like Coleridge, was a graduate of Cambridge in holy orders. He had been senior mathematical master at the Royal Institution School at Liverpool, and his publication, *A Harmony of the Bible with Experimental Physical Science* (1869) reflects both his religious and scientific interests. Rigg's heart lay in laboratories and workshops, and under his guidance the middle-class school became an outstanding science school. Both Henry Cole and Richard Redgrave of the Department of Science and Art sent sons to the school, and many of its former pupils won distinction in the scientific and medical worlds.

The training college itself was characterized by the large amount of work of a practical nature. Students played a major part in the actual building of the college chapel: quarrying stone and carving wood. They were each taught a trade: cabinet-making, bookbinding, leatherwork. Thus, as teachers, they would be skilled in industrial occupations.

Chester, however, was hard hit by the Revised Code. Student numbers fell to five, and in 1869 Rigg resigned in despair, only to see the training college revitalized by the demand for teachers following the 1870 Act. His vision of teachers recruited from industrial and commercial backgrounds and trained in a scientific and industrial milieu was lost.

In 1847 HMI Moseley wrote of the Chester students that 'They are generally robust and athletic men, four of whom would, I should think, weigh as much as five at Battersea and six at St Mark's' (Rich, 1972, p 83). The effect of centralized control of teacher training, however, was to standardize the product in the Battersea mould.

When William Taylor penned his delightful vignette of college-of-education life in the early 1970s (Taylor, 1984, pp 18–19), he stated that such a basic programme and culture of teacher education would have been recognizable to anyone who had worked in this area in the past 50 years. Taylor wrote of the 'emphasis on pastoral care; a residential tradition . . . awareness of the social and moral responsibilities of teachers', and noted the 'anxiety about the dangers of academicism . . . fears about the limitations of over-emphasizing relevance and the practical', and a 'vision of the world that viewed technological advance with some scepticism.'

Such a programme and culture, however, had a much longer pedigree.

It stemmed from the 1850s and 1860s, and reflected the victory of the curriculum and values of Kay-Shuttleworth over those of Coleridge and Rigg.

Educational theory

In 1888 the final report of the Cross Commission urged the establishment of some day training facilities in universities and university colleges. This recommendation won swift approval from the government, and in May 1890 Circular 287 set out detailed procedures governing the establishment and conduct of these new institutions. Though they were not required to follow the Education Department's syllabuses or examinations as such, each was to have a 'normal master or mistress', one of whose duties would be to lecture on the history and theory of education.

It should be noted that although students in university education departments (the term day training college soon became inappropriate with the establishment of residences and hostels) were allowed from the first to attend other lectures of the university, and a small number took degrees, they were essentially being prepared to teach in elementary schools. Even in 1925–6 there were 4,602 students in the university sector preparing for elementary teaching as opposed to only 917 for secondary.

Initially a two-year course was envisaged, but as early as 1891 provision was made for a one-year course for graduates and others with advanced university qualifications. At the same time a three-year course was made available for those intending both to graduate and to qualify as teachers. The first provision for a four-year course was made in 1911, and in 1926 the three-year concurrent course was finally abolished. Thereafter, students in this sector either took a three-year degree course followed by one year of professional study, or entered as graduates and took the one-year course. In 1926–7 there were 4,907 four-year students who had made the decision to become a teacher at the same time as they became undergraduates, and 499 one-year students. In 1938–9 the respective figures were 4,558 and 670 (Tuck, 1973a, p 92). After the Second World War, when unconditional grants became available for undergraduates, the four-year course which had required students, to take the 'pledge' that they would teach in elementary schools as a condition of grant, became irrelevant. It was finally abolished in 1951 (Gordon, 1986, p 90).

Education students with their guaranteed funding were a welcome addition to many hard-pressed university colleges and universities, and six departments were in operation by September 1890. By 1902 there were some 20, providing more than a quarter of the 5,000 students in training in England and Wales.

Though elementary training and non-graduate work f
the early years, the development of education as an aca
was recognized by the establishment of university cha⁞
In 1876 an example had already been provided in
most appropriately, money from the bequests of Andrew ⅃⁔
of the pioneers of monitorial schooling – was used to establish chairs
in education at the universities of Edinburgh and St Andrews.

Education chairs at Aberystwyth in 1893 and Bangor in 1894 were
followed by Newcastle in 1895, Manchester and Liverpool in 1899, and
the London Day Training College (from 1932 the Institute of Education)
in 1902. King's College, London, Birmingham and Exeter all followed
suit in 1903 (Tuck, 1973a, pp 82–3). Many of the holders of these early
chairs were historians of education: Foster Watson at Aberystwyth, W
H Woodward at Liverpool, J W Adamson at King's, London. In the
inter-war period, when four more departments were established – at
Swansea, Durham, Leicester and Hull – new professorial appointments
included a significant number of psychologists.

Educational theory developed in several ways. By the 1960s philosophical, sociological and comparative studies had emerged as separate
disciplines of education, alongside history and psychology (Tuck,
1973b). Such specialization made the applicability of educational theory
to initial teacher education increasingly problematic, particularly on one-
year courses (Hirst, 1985; Sutherland, 1985). At the same time there was
an increase in the theoretical studies surrounding the teaching of specific
subjects. Though subsequent changes cannot be examined in detail here,
and fall within the province of other chapters in this book, some basic
historical conclusions in respect of the relationship between educational
theory and initial teacher education may be drawn.

The study of education in an academic or theoretical way is potentially
a valuable exercise, both for those individuals who engage in it, and for
society more generally. To take a first degree in education, with no
immediate commitment to becoming a teacher or engagement in any
professional preparation, is at least as important an activity as taking
a first degree in history, geography, sociology, classics or English
literature. Such undergraduate studies, however, never developed in
this country in any coherent way.

Three- and four-year courses were originally devised for students who
were committed to teach in elementary schools. University departments
gained in status in one sense when, after the Second World War, they
concentrated on one-year postgraduate courses. In the 1950s and 1960s,
their students were themselves products of grammar or independent
schools, who intended to teach in similar establishments. There was
still room in such courses for some study of educational theory.

.eparation by means of a one-year postgraduate course for teaching primary or secondary comprehensive schools, however, signalled the end of the theory-before-practice approach to initial teacher education. School-centred, school-based approaches were favoured by the Secretary of State, by HMI, by the Council for the Accreditation of Teacher Education (CATE), by teachers, and by students themselves. In consequence educational theory has largely disappeared from one-year courses.

Conclusion

The historical perspective shows that changing methods in the preparation of teachers have often reflected broader changes in educational institutions, standards and theory. For example at the beginning of the nineteenth century there were only two universities in England and Wales, and for that reason (and many others) there was no possibility of an all-graduate school teaching force. Such a development would require a massive expansion of higher education, and the recognition of the graduate status of teacher-training colleges and of their courses, changes which did not occur until the 1960s. Thus the attainment of an all-graduate teaching profession was dependent on the development of mass secondary schooling and higher education, and in particular upon the admission of girls and women to these areas. Increasing numbers of graduates also dramatically altered the balance of training between Certificate/B Ed and PGCE courses. Acceptances to initial training courses in England and Wales saw the concurrent:consecutive course ratio shift from 6.8:1 in 1966 to 0.6:1 in 1980 (Bruce, 1985, p 166)

On the other hand, many changes in teacher education have stemmed directly from factors outside the educational sphere. Thus in the 1860s economic and political considerations in the period after the Crimean War led to retrenchment in government educational expenditure, a determination to reduce the status of teachers, and a consequent decrease in the numbers of pupil teachers and of students in training. The Education Act of 1870, however, which was based in part upon the new social and political philosophy expressed in the extension of the franchise in 1867, necessitated the provision of many more qualified teachers. In the short term, nevertheless, standards of entry were relaxed to allow such an increase to take place. Similarly, the Second World War produced a great teacher shortage, so that emergency schemes of training were instituted, some of only one term's duration. Between 1944 and 1951 some 35,000 ex-servicemen and women were trained under the Emergency Recruitment and Training of Teachers Scheme (Bruce, 1985, p 165).

In 1990 there is another teacher shortage. This is the product of a flight by teachers from the classroom, so that there are probably more qualified teachers outside schools than inside. Such a failure to proceed into, or stay in teaching, is a product of the low status and pay of teachers in comparison with similarly qualified people in other professions.

Low status and pay have prompted a search for new sources of teachers, and the introduction of new apprenticeship methods of training for graduates and others with a minimum of two years' higher education. Whether such 'articled' and 'licensed' teachers will come to bear the same reputation as the nineteenth-century pupil teachers – seen as substitutes for 'proper' teachers – remains to be seen.

In the 1990s it seems essential, if teacher education is indeed to evolve, rather than to regress, for the following lessons to be drawn from history.

Although no single method of teacher education is equally applicable to all recruits to the profession, elements of apprenticeship, training and educational theory should all be included.

Apprenticeship has a fundamental role to play. Teaching is in many ways a highly practical activity. Learning on the job under the guidance of a skilled practitioner who has the responsibility and time to initiate the student into the skills of class management and control is a most important element in learning to teach. Nevertheless it should be recognized that, by itself, apprenticeship is an inadequate means of preparation for a professional occupation.

Students need to generalize from their specific situations. This necessitates attendance at training institutions where they can make contact with other students and trainers from outside the particular classroom and school. In their training institutions they should also make some initial contact with education as an intellectual discipline. Teachers should be educated persons, and recognizable as such in the community, not least in respect of the subject of education itself.

The formula for improving the quality of teachers and teaching is thus twofold. In the first place the best features of apprenticeship, training and theory should be incorporated into a coherent whole. These must be carried through into what is at present (often euphemistically) called the probationary year, and beyond. No other major profession has so short a period of training and induction as do teachers.

Secondly, good teachers should be retained within the classroom. On several occasions over the last 150 years, the standards of entry into teaching have been lowered, because without such a lowering certain groups of children would have remained untaught. At present it is primarily the responsibility of the Secretary of State for Education to ensure that the conditions of teaching, in terms of status and pay, are such as to encourage sufficient good-quality recruits to join and remain within teaching. If that task cannot be satisfactorily undertaken by central government it should be handed over to a general teaching council.

Though articled-teacher schemes and other forms of on-the-job training may, in the short term, bring more people into classrooms they will not in themselves improve the quality of teaching and of education. As HM Senior Chief Inspector recently reported – and his words reflect the judgements of HMI across 150 years of educational history – circumstances may well produce a '"never mind the quality, feel the width" attitude. Standards of learning are never improved by poor teachers and there are no cheap, high-quality routes into teaching' (Department of Education and Science, 1989a, para 70).

Chapter 2

Teacher Education Today

Michael Naish

Introduction: near the bull's eye

In describing 'teacher education today', there is an inherent danger that what is written will be out of date by the time of publication. Teacher education is currently susceptible to rapid and radical change. With an unshakeable majority and intent on effecting social change, the Conservative government of the 1980s has, understandably, taken education as a prime target for attention. Since teacher education presumably affects the quality and professional ability of teachers in schools, through both initial and in-service teacher education, this area of activity has been perceived as fairly near the bull's eye of that particular target.

It follows that this attempt to describe initial teacher education in England and Wales at the beginning of a new decade can only produce a snapshot in time. The 1980s have seen very significant changes in initial teacher education, including, for example, improved links between tertiary institutions and schools through the development of the concept of 'partnership' and the process of vetting courses within a set of centrally imposed criteria (see Chapters 1, 4 and 7).

Perhaps the most confident prediction about initial teacher education is that, in the 1990s we are likely to see still more fundamental changes. Some of these changes may be developments of those initiated in the 1980s; others may surprise us all. The pressures exerted by teacher shortages, for example, could lead to unpredicted responses from administrations under stress. Even if there is a change of government, we may well find that the assumption of centralized control of education, skilfully managed through the 1980s, is unlikely to be relaxed as the 1990s unfold. Inertia alone may be sufficient to ensure this.

Places and numbers

Courses of initial teacher training (ITT), are available in institutes of higher education, polytechnics and university departments of education. Students train to be teachers through one of two possible routes: the Bachelor of Education (BEd) or the Postgraduate Certificate of Education (PGCE). Both routes take four years, the BEd most commonly in a single institution. For the PGCE, students complete their first degree in a particular discipline or, more rarely, through an interdisciplinary course. Then, to qualify for the PGCE, they commonly move to a different institution for their postgraduate course.

A major difference between the BEd and the PGCE routes is that concepts, issues and skills concerned with education may be constructively integrated with subject studies in the four-year BEd, while the first degree course (or further studies) of the PGCE student may have been totally unrelated to such matters. Thus, while the BEd student has time for concepts to be acquired and skills developed, the PGCE student has 36 weeks in which to grapple with the demanding task. The task is compounded by the need to confront unfamiliar concepts, develop new skills and cope with the physical and emotional demands of school experience, all of which ought, at least in theory, to be competently and effectively handled in the more expansive time-scale of the BEd course.

Yet, despite these pressures on the one-year course, the PGCE route became the dominant one in terms of numbers in the 1980s, with roughly equal intake of BEd and PGCE numbers by the end of the decade. In 1989, 20,548 students were recruited for initial teacher education courses. Of these, 10,088 were admitted to BEd and 10,460 to PGCE courses. Of the PGCE students, 5,527 were in university departments of education (with 1,274 training for primary schools and 4,253 for secondary). The remaining 4,933 were in colleges and institutes of higher education and polytechnics, with 2,806 primary and 2,127 secondary.

These figures show great contrasts with the 1960s and 1970s. In 1972, the numbers of students admitted to ITT courses in England and Wales reached a peak at 50,623, more than double those in the early sixties (26,261 in 1963). In the early and mid-sixties, the three-year Teacher's Certificate was the main route and this was offered in colleges of education. The PGCE at that time was available almost exclusively in the universities and was mainly concerned with preparing specialist subject teachers for work in selective secondary schools.

In the late 1960s and early seventies, three- and four-year BEd courses were introduced. The Teacher's Certificate was not phased out until after 1979. But after 1973, the demographic trend – that is, the decline in the birth rate – took its toll of the colleges, which were reorganized into institutes and colleges of higher education. The toll included the closure of colleges and redundancy, redeployment or early retirement of staff.

Meanwhile, PGCE courses were becoming more widespread in their distribution, being available in institutes of higher education and polytechnics as well as university departments of education. The PGCE was also changing in character as courses responded to the demands of comprehensive schools and as postgraduate courses to prepare students for primary-school teaching were introduced. By the 1980s, more students were admitted to PGCE courses than to BEd courses.

Given the current ideological preference of the government for 'adademic standards' as expressed in the specialist study involved in a single-subject first degree, it seems likely that the PGCE route, with a 'training' year tacked on to the three years of academic study, will continue to be favoured in the increasingly centralized system of ITT.

Style of courses

In broadest terms, the content of initial-teacher-education courses is based on four major elements: one dealing with the process of teaching; a second with what may be loosely called 'educational theory'; the third with practical experience of teaching in schools, that is 'teaching practice'; and the fourth concerned with 'subject studies'.

For BEd students, as was the case for the Certificate of Education students of the past, the subject studies are normally based on the study of a main and a second, or subsidiary, subject. The subject-based course is continued over the full extent of the course: three years for the old Certificate of Education and four years for the BEd. PGCE students, on the other hand, normally complete their subject studies during the three-year course that leads to the award of their Bachelor or first degree.

The 'process of teaching' part is often called 'methods work', but this expression is not particularly helpful since it suggests a very mechanistic approach to the business of teaching children. Much more valuable is the other commonly employed term, 'curriculum studies'. This expression helps conjure up the image of courses which are considering the whole notion of curriculum, including aims, objectives, operations, pedagogy, evaluation and assessment rather than the apparently unproblematic and rather simplistic business of 'methods'. 'Curriculum' should also

(Based on Bell, 1981 and commentary in Furlong et al, 1988)

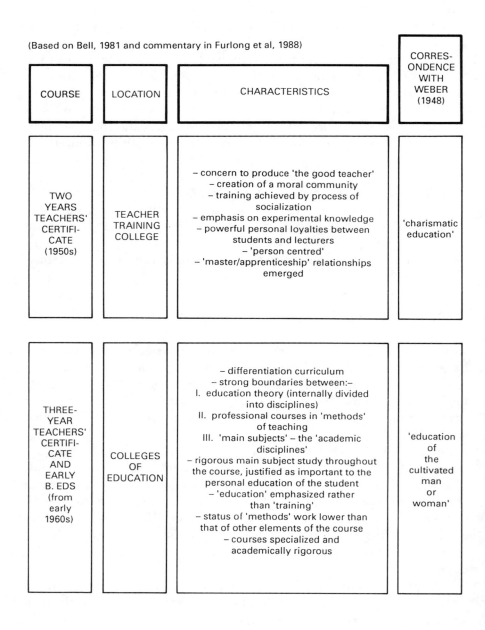

Figure 2.1   *Changing courses, changing philosophies*

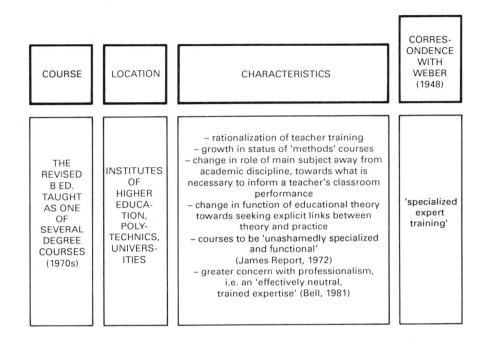

COURSE	LOCATION	CHARACTERISTICS	CORRES-ONDENCE WITH WEBER (1948)
THE REVISED B ED. TAUGHT AS ONE OF SEVERAL DEGREE COURSES (1970s)	INSTITUTES OF HIGHER EDUCA-TION, POLY-TECHNICS, UNIVERS-ITIES	– rationalization of teacher training – growth in status of 'methods' courses – change in role of main subject away from academic discipline, towards what is necessary to inform a teacher's classroom performance – change in function of educational theory towards seeking explicit links between theory and practice – courses to be 'unashamedly specialized and functional' (James Report, 1972) – greater concern with professionalism, i.e. an 'effectively neutral, trained expertise' (Bell, 1981)	'specialized expert training'

Figure 2.1 *(continued)*

help suggest that the children have a somewhat more active part to play in the process than those who are simply subjected to 'methods'.

The 'educational theory' element of courses of initial teacher education draws from what used to be called 'the foundation disciplines' – mainly sociology, psychology, philosophy and history, but with contributions also from areas such as comparative education. The teaching-practice element is integrated into courses in a variety of ways.

Bell's (1981) descriptive model of Teachers' Certificate and BEd courses between the 1950s and late 1970s provides a valuable framework for reflection on the nature of current ITT courses. He recognized three broad phases, coinciding with changes in nomenclature from 'Teacher Training Colleges', through 'Colleges of Education' to 'Institutes and Colleges of Higher Education'. Each phase, according to Bell, had characteristic culture, structure, organization of knowledge and ways of social interaction; he postulated that these showed a certain level of correspondence with Weber's (1948) three ideal types of education: 'charismatic education', 'education of the cultivated man or woman' and 'specialized expert training'.

Bell's model of teacher education from the 1950s to the 1970s is summarized in figure 2.1. Bell was concerned with Teacher's Certificate and BEd courses, but Furlong et al (1988) demonstrate certain parallels between BEd and PGCE courses. They suggest that until the mid-1970s there was a focus on 'the educated man or woman' in PGCE courses, but that there was strong differentiation between 'methods' and 'educational theory'. The latter was 'legitimated' as academic knowledge enshrined within disciplines and was perceived as having higher status than the more functional methods work. Students gained preparation in their institutions and practised application in schools on teaching practice. The educational disciplines were thought to be an important element in the preparation stages.

In recent years, as Furlong et al (1988) point out, PGCE courses have moved towards the promotion of 'specialized expert training' in line with other ITT courses and with the requirements of centralized policy through CATE (The Council for the Accreditation of Teacher Education) (see Chapter 7).

Bell's framework must be accepted as a model, with the limitations that this implies, but it does provide us with a useful context for the consideration of current courses. It raises the very important issue of where courses should be placed on continua between, for example, 'cultural and instrumental'; 'education and training'; 'humanistic and enterprise focused'.

Teaching quality and CATE

The notion of 'specialized expert training' is signalled in the very language currently used in teacher-education circles, as was suggested in Bell's model. Initial courses are now referred to as initial teacher *training* and the broader, more humanistic notion of teacher *education* is excluded through the use of such terminology.

The very focus of 'the great debate' on education, initiated in 1976, was the quality of what was provided; questions about quality inevitably lead to others about accountability. Accountability may be measured against sets of criteria and it was no surprise that the government's White Paper on teaching quality (Department of Education and Science, 1983b), placed emphasis on the notion of training rather than educating teachers and proposed that in future courses would have to meet a set of specified criteria.

Drawing largely on the advice of the Advisory Committee on the Supply and Education of Teachers (ACSET), a set of criteria was drawn up and in Circular 3/84 (Department of Education and Science, 1984) the establishment of the Council for the Accreditation of Teacher Education (CATE) was announced. The role of CATE would be to advise the Secretaries of State for Education and for Wales on the approval of initial teacher training (sic) courses in England and Wales. First a review was to be undertaken of existing courses, making use of reports based on visits of Her Majesty's Inspectorate (HMI). Each institution was required to establish a Local Committee for Teacher Education, with representation from local education authorities, practising school teachers and individuals from outside the education service, in addition to members of the institution. CATE would then make recommendations about approval or non-approval of courses to the Secretaries of State based on the evidence from HMI and submissions made by the institutions. The support of the local committee was to be essential for approval of courses to be given.

A revised and developed set of criteria emerged from consideration of the first round of accreditation in Circular 24/89 in November 1989 (Department of Education and Science, 1989b) and in future, local committees are to serve consortia of at least three institutions each. These new local committees will take on some of the accreditation responsibility of the central CATE.

It is interesting to note that the original criteria largely reflected developing practice in initial teacher education, so that for institutions concerned with continuing development of the curricula of their courses, CATE did not impose drastic changes. For others, the level and impact of change must have been more dramatic.

A case study: the PGCE, Institute of Education, University of London

At this stage it may be helpful to consider an example of a course in initial teacher education to provide a case study through which to reflect upon the range and variety of practice elsewhere. The case in point is the course with which the writer is most familiar, having been involved in its development and currently responsible for its management.

The current PGCE course at the Institute of Education was first taught in the 1985–6 session. It is broadly based on proposals made in a report of a working party on the structure and examination of the PGCE, called *Partnership and Opportunity* and produced in November 1983. The detailed planning of the course was undertaken by a planning committee and an education component committee. The course is kept under continuous review by a PGCE review committee, which reports to the Initial Courses Board of the Institute.

The broad characteristics of the course

In broadest terms, the institute of education PGCE course sets out to:

- be effective in preparing beginning teachers for their professional tasks;
- be relevant to current and future needs and practice in schools and colleges;
- encourage students to be aware of issues and problem in contemporary education and to clarify their own position with respect to such issues.
- encourage students to build on their professional and personal development through continuing in-service work.

In order to work towards the achievement of these broad purposes, the structure of the course is designed to facilitate a close, forward-looking partnership with schools and practising teachers. Through the involvement of teachers, tutors and students in this partnership, opportunities are created to discuss and investigate issues and problems as and when they arise from school experience. In this way it is hoped that there will be a close integration of theory with practice. The pedagogy is based on active, enquiry learning, together with constructive self-evaluation; the assessment system is intended to reflect the nature of the course and encourage its evaluation and development.

Broad aims

The PGCE course aims primarily to provide a coherent professional education and training, which integrates practical experiences and learning of theory. In order to achieve this, it is intended that the course will enable students to understand the nature of the change involved in making the transformation from student to teacher. Thus the course sets out to alert the students to the intellectual, affective, social, historical and political dimensions of the task they are to undertake. That task is to educate people for life in our changing, multicultural society, and the context for this is a dynamic world of limited renewable resources and fragile environments.

The course is also intended to provide supportive learning structures that are sensitive to the position of students undertaking initial professional education and the requirements of the student as professional teacher. We therefore aim to take students personal and professional growth as a focus and hence provide them with opportunities for the realization of such growth.

More specific aims

The course planners broke down the set of broad aims into more specific aims, which would be more helpful in actually putting the course into operation. These were as follows:

- Skills and abilities

   Teaching requires the acquisition of a range of skills. In order to be effective, these skills have to be woven into habitual action patterns. Teachers at the beginning of their careers need to be inducted into the basic skills of teaching so as to provide the foundation for further skill development. The course sets out to involve students in developing a range of skills concerned with organizing an environment and climate conducive to learning, such as:

   - stimulating and fostering children's interests;
   - organizing children's learning experiences;
   - evaluating their own work and that of the children;
   - contributing towards course planning;
   - communicating effectively with children, colleagues, parents and the public at large;
   - handling and managing educational hardware, including recent technology.

- Knowledge and understanding

Beginning teachers need to consider what the education system *is* like and *ought* to be like. They should be required to ask normative questions about what *ought* to happen and should be helped, through study and observation, to find out what *is* actually happening. They ought to be encouraged to go on to seek explanations for any discrepancies observed.

The course encourages students to develop knowledge and understanding of:

- theory relevant to the needs of the beginning teacher;
- the education system, its recent development and future trends;
- general characteristics of the curriculum, its constraints and opportunities;
- the aims and educational potential of their subject or specialism and its relationship with the broader curriculum;
- methods of planning and teaching learning sequences which involve children in the process of learning;
- methods of evaluating and assessing children's work;
- broad educational problems and issues.

● Personal qualities

The course sets out to foster and encourage certain characteristics of a good teacher. It highlights those qualities most pertinent to effective teaching and encourages students to shape these in a specifically educational manner by building on relevant skills and understanding. Such qualities include:

- concern for children and for society;
- professional commitment;
- openness and sensitivity to change;
- a disposition towards cooperation with colleagues in a common drive for the enhancement of children's education;
- the ability to respond sensitively and constructively to children and colleagues.

Structure of the course

The course has four main elements: school experience, curriculum studies, the education component (called 'Issues in Education') and further professional option (FPO).

School experience

School experience includes school visits, school-based days in curriculum work and teaching practice. School-based days focus on the curriculum studies work, but also feed into 'Issues in Education'. They are timetabled for one day per week in Terms 1 and 2, but in the summer term, more flexible arrangements are made and school-based work may extend to at least two days a week. Block teaching practice consists of two weeks of preliminary experience in a primary school, and two main blocks of teaching practice during the course. It is felt that a period of time in the Institute between these two main blocks is essential for the development of the students' teaching and management skills.

During school-based days, curriculum tutors work in schools and colleges with school staff, students and children. Students are engaged in a range of activities which may include, for example, small group teaching, team teaching, full class work, micro teaching, use of sound and video to record teaching, planning work, observation of classes, evaluation of lessons, observation and involvement in tutor periods or form time, observation of assembly, fieldwork, consideration of whole-school planning, and discussion of questions and issues arising out of the experience. Students share in planning, teaching, evaluation and pastoral work with staff, colleagues and tutors. Fundamentally they gain experience of classroom and school life in a realistic manner. Their experience is concrete and at first hand rather than abstract and removed to a second-hand source.

Experience of this nature, based in and concerned with schools and centred on the teaching of the student's main curriculum or age-phase area, is a vital component of initial training whatever the particular requirements of the student's specialist subject. It acknowledges the crucial notion that all subject teachers are involved primarily in educating children in schools and that their subject is a medium for education rather than an end in its own right.

For the main teaching practice, the Institute set out to develop a system of 'partnership' schools with clear and recognized commitment to teacher-education links with the Institute. Three or four students would be allocated to each school; within each school, the subject teachers concerned, together with a designated teacher tutor with overall responsibility for initial training within the school, would work with Institute tutors and the students to cover a range of subjects.

In addition to normal teaching practice supervision, Institute tutors would act as link tutors, one for each partnership school, and would visit the school at least once a term and develop the relationship between the school and the Institute across a range of priorities.

It was felt that the advantages of the partnership system would include:

- students being supportive of each other in school;
- teacher-tutors and subject teachers working as a coordinated team;
- seminars held on site, involving students, school staff and Institute tutors;
- students from three of four schools forming an education group for work on 'issues in education';
- education tutors being involved in school experience, since their students are placed in only three or four schools;
- teacher tutors and/or subject teachers freed to attend, organize and contribute to Institute-based sessions;
- teacher tutors in the schools being able to coordinate their ITT work with other aspects of teacher education such as induction of new staff, probationary year support, staff development and in-service work.

In addition to these arrangements for school experience, a number of practising teachers are involved in the PGCE either as part-time tutors – particularly in 'Issues in Education' – or as visiting tutors. The visiting tutors scheme had been in operation, with support from the local authorities, for some years before the current course was developed. The Institute invites experienced teachers from schools with which it is closely connected, to help in the work of its subject department and to share the supervision of students on teaching practice. Tutors assist for the equivalent of half a day per week and normally serve for a maximum of two years. In many departments visiting tutors play an important part in work undertaken for the school-based day. In others, activities may include taking part in tutorials, holding tutorials, workshops or seminars, lecturing or becoming involved in any activity which will complement the work from the perspective of the practising teacher.

Curriculum studies
The curriculum-studies element of the course is concerned with the development of teaching skills relating mainly to a curriculum subject or subjects for secondary students or to an age-phase for primary. They are also concerned with theories of teaching and learning and with general curriculum issues. It is intended that theory and practice should also be integrated. Students are asked, at secondary and FE level, to consider the nature of their subject: what it has to offer to the education of young people; how that contribution may be planned and constructed into a curriculm; how children learn within the framework of a subject or cross-disciplinary area; how best to develop pedagogy; how the work may be evaluated and assessed. At primary level, students

have to make similar considerations across the full range of subjects in the primary curriculum.

Two full days are available for curriculum work in non-teaching-practice time: one day is school-based and one is Institute-based in terms 1 and 2. Some work may, at secondary level, be based on a single subject; it may be part of a two-subject course, or it may be cross-disciplinary. The opportunity for close integration between school-based work and Institute-based work is clear. Time is allocated to methods work on teaching practice on Fridays in term 1.

For primary students, all subjects of the primary curriculum are included in curriculum work. At the end of the first week of term, students make a choice of age-phase specialization between early years (3–8) and middle years (7–12). The further professional option for primary students enables them to select a particular curriculum area for a special focus, from science, mathematics, language, art and design, social studies/humanities, music, community languages or nursery. This is seen as a first step in developing the dual role of primary teachers as responsible not only for the work of a class across the entire range of the curriculum, but also as coordinators in one, sometimes broad, curriculum area.

Further professional options

At secondary and FE level too, all students study a further professional option (FPO). It was felt that there is a danger in the one-year PGCE that much of the work may remain at a superficial level simply through pressure of time and that it would therefore be helpful to introduce options which would allow study in depth of an additional teaching subject or a special-interest area. Students select one FPO from a list of about 25 for secondary and from the list mentioned above for primary.

The criteria for the FPO are that they should provide students with a further professional accomplishment that they can take with them into their first posts. The FPOs should integrate theory with practice rather than be purely theoretical or purely practical. They should be amenable to work undertaken by students in their school experience and they should pay attention to the needs of whole-school policies. Examples at secondary level include computer-assisted learning in the humanities and in the sciences; drama and theatre arts; exercise and fitness education; gender and education; race, culture and education; special educational needs; the teaching of history, RE, English.

Issues in education

The education component of the Institute PGCE focuses on a critical examination of classroom, school and societal issues based on relevant theory and practical knowledge. This is an issues-based course, which

PGCE COURSE WORK ASSESSMENT CRITERIA

1. Experience, reading and reflection

(a) Does the assignment demonstrate the student's ability to draw together personal experience, reading and reflection as a basis for her or his professional and personal development?

(b) Are connections made between various elements of the course (i.e. school experience, FPO, curriculum, education), recognized and used where appropriate?

2. Educational argument

(a) Does the assignment demonstrate the development of clear and logical argument about education matters?

(b) Is the argument well structured?

(c) Is the argument grounded in appropriate evidence?

(d) Are the student's own views expressed where appropriate?

3. Theory and practice

(a) Are appropriate examples of theory and practice used to illustrate points made?

(b) Is the relationship between theory and practice carefully considered with respect to the topic under discussion?

4. Reporting enquiry

Where an enquiry undertaken by the student at first hand is reported, does the report:–

(a) discuss the practical, ethical and intellectual problems and advantages of the enquiry (e.g. collecting the data, evaluating the data, analysis and reporting),

(b) show ability to evaluate the status of the conclusions?

Figure 2.2   *Institute of Education, University of London*

encourages students to explore the range of values and attitudes involved in the issues and to clarify their own position in the light of analysis and discussion. They are, as already suggested, encouraged to analyse normative questions, about what *ought* to be, as well as empirical questions about the nature of the actual conditions and situation. Their studies take them on to consider reasons for certain discrepancies and to suggest possible appropriate actions.

In order to facilitate this work, enquiry approaches are encouraged through the use of group work and resource materials, linked to a basic framework of presentations. Education groups containing about 15 students are normally made up from four or five teaching-practice schools in the secondary course. Students thus bring shared experiences to the group. Groups have the possibility of involving tutors from their schools and a range of perspectives from different subject areas is provided. Primary students remain in their curriculum groups for this component, but links between primary and secondary groups are made both formally and informally.

Each group is allocated an education tutor, who is responsible for organizing the issues in education work for students in her or his group. This is undertaken in consultation with the group. While each group covers the syllabus, there is considerable flexibility as to how this is achieved. Tutors have access to the teaching-practice schools in which their students are placed, thus providing the opportunity for establishing effective links.

Assessment

The assessment of students on the course is based on a practical element – their work in teaching practice – and a written element – two or three pieces of coursework. The coursework takes the form of assignments in curriculum, FPO and issues-in-education work. The curriculum assignment is a piece of work between 6,000 and 10,000 words, 4,000 of which may be in the form of a project – for example a curriculum package or a set of media resources. Assignments for the FPO and for issues in education are between 3,000 and 5,000 words each, or a combined study of between 6,000 and 10,000 words. Students and examiners work to a set of assessment criteria, as set out in Figure 2.2.

Evaluation

Evaluation has been meticulously carried out since the current course was initiated in 1985. Each element of the course has been evaluated by students and staff, as has the whole course. Generally a process of small group discussion and questionnaire survey has been employed to gather evaluative data. This careful evaluation has helped to develop the course in a variety of ways. For example, there has been direct feedback into the issues-in-education element and the format, programme and resource bank have been revised each year in response to evaluation. The same applies to other elements of the course.

Despite this careful review and development work, there remain certain questions about the course which warrant further consideration. It was anticipated, for example, that the four elements of the course would be seen as critically interlinked and that staff and students would make inter-connections between the elements. This has been difficult to achieve and evaluation still demonstrates that some students see the course as being made up of fairly discrete elements.

This problem also relates to the question of interdisciplinary and cross-curricular work. With a firm subject–department tradition in the Institute of Education and with students having specialized in particular subject-based degrees on the whole, it is difficult to initiate progressive cooperation across the curriculum. The hopes that the 'new' course, as it was called in 1985, would help to break down divisions between subjects, have not been realized as fully as they might have been.

The model of partnership schools with strong Institute links has also proved difficult to achieve as fully as was hoped. While good things have developed, the benefits are not as universal as anticipated and the scheme is, at the time of writing, ripe for review. Part of the problem lies in the heavy workloads which face both teachers in schools and tutors at the Institute, particularly since workloads have increased steeply to cope with the bureaucracy associated with a more centralized system of school and teacher education.

Work has been undertaken on all these points through the work of the PGCE Review Committee and the Initial Course Board. A continuing series of staff-development workshops is being carried through. These workshops have brought staff together across the Institute from a range of departments and interests and have gone some way to breaking down the subject barriers and opening up discussion of the PGCE curriculum. Topics for workshops have included interviews and admissions of PGCE students; managing school-based days; supervising teaching practice; making links across the course; language, education and the PGCE; multicultural and anti-racist education and the PGCE; the National Curriculum and the implications for the PGCE and so on.

Currently a very important opportunity for the ongoing development of the course is the Institute's involvement as a pilot institution in the TVEI in the initial-teacher-training initiative of the Training Agency. TVEI is the Technical and Vocational Education Initiative, sponsored centrally through the Training Agency, which has achieved considerable impact in schools and colleges and has recently been extended to each local education authority. The basic idea of the initiative is to enable institutions of ITT to explore the implications of TVEI and its extension phase for courses of initial teacher education. The focus is to be on staff development and, in the case of the Institute's pilot project, this is taken to imply that course development must follow.

Funding for this project has enabled the PGCE management team to set up some 13 tutor-led research projects relating to certain key foci of TVEI work, viz workplace learning, cross-curricular initiatives, modular course structures, active learning and assessment. In addition, a pilot profiling scheme has been established. This involves six curriculum tutor groups for secondary/FE and the whole of the primary group in developing a profiling, or records of achievement experiment through the course of the 1989–90 session.

Students build up a portfolio of their work and maintain a diary, which may be personal to them if they so wish. The diary is intended to work as a self-learning device and a means of critical reflection on the course and its impacts. It seems likely, at the time of writing, that the scheme may lead to students going into their first teaching posts equipped with examples of their work and a record of their achievements together with an indication of where they most need support during induction and the probationary period. This record will have been developed through negotiation between the student, her or his Institute tutors and the school or college tutor. It should provide a framework for the continuing professional development of the student.

While these experimental developments are taking place, the project is also providing the opportunity for a more general consideration of the structures of the course in the light of five years of experience and evaluation and within the context of the implications of TVEI in schools and colleges. In order to initiate this course review and development, 25 tutors recently spent two days on a residential in-house conference. This took place in a hotel some miles from London, so that tutors could focus clearly on the task in hand, untroubled by the daily demands of life within the Institution.

A further development for the Institute of Education PGCE is involvement in the Articled Teachers Scheme. This is another centrally funded initiative, this time through the Department of Education and Science. The scheme is to trial two-year PGCE courses for students who are to be maintained through a bursary over the two years. The course will be essentially school-based, with students spending four-fifths of their time in school and one-fifth in the teacher education institution. Successful students obtain the PGCE qualification and Qualified Teacher Status at the end of the course. Some 16 consortia of institutions and local authorities are due to commence the pilot courses in September 1990.

General trends

The case study illustrates certain trends in initial teacher education that are common across many courses and reflect both the conventional wisdom acquired as well as the requirements of CATE criteria. One of the dominant trends is the movement towards more pragmatic approaches: the 'specialized expert training' approach as explored in Bell's model. Thus the courses have built in more school-based work and have developed the notion of effective involvement of practising teachers through partnership schemes and school-based initiatives.

Furlong et al (1988) have explored what is involved in such partnership links and provide useful evaluative case studies of schemes at the universities of Leicester, for a primary course, and Sussex, for a secondary. School-based approaches have since been developed further at Oxford University, through building in continuous school work throughout the PGCE year and developing the complementary roles of tutors in the university, 'interns' (the students working in schools) and 'mentors', (the teachers formally involved in the scheme) through negotiation with the school and the local education authority. School-based approaches and partnership may well be further developed by the Articled Teachers Scheme, described above.

A second significant trend, clearly illustrated by the case study, has been the rethinking of the relationship between theory and practice. This is linked to the requirement for a more pragmatic approach. The impact of the trend has been to move away from a systematic input from the educational disciplines of psychology, sociology, philosophy and history, towards the more issue-based approach illustrated by the issues-in-education element of the Institute of Education PGCE described in the case study.

To some extent this was a pragmatic decision based on the problem of students trying to grapple with a range of concepts from a number of disciplines during a short period of study when their priorities are more to do with the question of managing children's learning in a practical situation. In a four-year BEd course, the pressures are not quite so severe and there may well be more time and opportunity for students to develop meaningful learning in the disciplines. This certainly seems to be the case if one compares students from the two routes in MA classes in education. BEd students frequently display a more advanced level of conceptual understanding of elements of the educational disciplines than do those who entered teaching through the PGCE route. This assertion, however, really needs further research exploration if it is to be stated with confidence.

Finally, a third significant current trend to be noted is the interest in profiling as applied to students undertaking courses in initial teacher education. Most teacher-education courses have always included an element of profiling in the practical assessment, which was based on a number of criteria forming a profile of the candidate's performance. In the light of work on profiles and records of achievement in schools and colleges, this work is now being explored more carefully and with promising results. The main benefits may well turn out to be more to do with learning and self-reflection than with assessment.

These dominant trends in initial teacher education have been derived from the case study given above of the PGCE course in one individual institution. For an overview of ITT courses in the public sector – the colleges and institutes of higher education – see *Quality in Schools. The Initial Training of Teachers*, (Department of Education and Science, 1987), which provides valuable information on the situation before the true impact of CATE could be assessed. The book presents the findings of a survey undertaken by HMI between January 1983 and January 1985. In 1988, HMI provided a perspective on ITT in the university departments, this time based on their experience of visiting such institutions in order to report to CATE (Department of Education and Science, 1988). The programme of visits began in the autumn of 1982 and the booklet summarizes the findings of 29 such visits.

Conclusion

Teacher education in the 1990s finds itself under pressure. There are the general problems concerned with funding which affect universities, polytechnics and institutes and colleges of higher education as a whole. The impact of reduced funding has directly threatened the very existence of some university departments of education.

The impact of CATE is seen by many as of increasing significance and there is talk of the possibility of the imposition from 'above' of a national curriculum for teacher education. Some see the criteria and their explication in Circular 24/89 as *in effect* a national curriculum for teacher education (Department of Education and Science, 1989b)

Tutors in institutions providing teacher courses in initial teacher education find themselves, in the face of these funding difficulties and the requirements of CATE, pressed for time. This is a particular problem in the universities, where the individual research of lecturers and larger-scale funded research is of increasing importance, not only for its intrinsic value, but also because it is used as a yardstick against which funding is measured. It is difficult for a tutor engaged fully in initial teacher education to fulfil research requirements, write and publish successfully and take a fare share of administrative and committee work. The fact is that promotion in the university sector depends more on research and writing than on teaching. It is to be hoped that the students do not suffer in these circumstances.

Add to all this the fact that teachers are leaving the profession due to low morale, poor public image and low salaries. There are also signs that recruitment on to teacher-education courses may become increasingly difficult, particularly in the nineties, when the number of young people of 'initial teacher education age' will dramatically decline due to the demographic change. Given these circumstances it is clear that it will take a major effort of will, professionalism and idealism for the quality of initial teacher education to be maintained and further developed through the decade.

Chapter 3

Teacher Education: A Comparative View

Robert Cowen

Introduction: bringing chickens home to roost

Comparative educationists are often asked where the fields are greener: that is, which other countries are doing something in education better than we are? The probability that other countries are indeed doing something better in education is now part of the public discourse of English politicians and the mass media. Comparisons in education are useful, or so it seems.

Comparative educationists are also sometimes asked: how can we borrow those good practices? This second question – *how* can we borrow – is a bit rarer, perhaps because of the assumption that education is like a technology and, with only small difficulty, internationally transferable.

However, there is a large literature in comparative education devoted to showing that education is not a simple transferable technology. The theoretical anxieties about international transferability go back to at least the turn of this century, when Sir Michael Sadler answered most cautiously his own question, 'How far can we learn anything of practical value from the study of foreign educational systems?' Even more cautious answers to that question were worked out during the 1920s and 1930s by scholars such as Hans, Hessen and Kandel, who offered different approaches to the analysis of national cultures. But they all recognized that educational ideas and practices taken from, or metaphorically torn from, the social contexts in which they had been created, were unlikely to succeed in other countries.

In 1990, despite sustained effort (such as the methodological work of G Z F Bereday, N Hans, B Holmes, I Kandel, E J King, J Lauwerys, and V Mallinson), there is still no widely accepted general theory which defines just what aspects of (any two or more) historical, economic and cultural contexts will assist, block or subvert the solution which is to be brought home from abroad. The confidence of persons in public life, stressing the benefits of their particular instant solution from overseas (comprehensive schools, polytechnical education, magnet schools, competency-based teacher education) is very rarely matched by similar optimism among specialists in the university.

Comparative education is not, then, 'Useful' in the simple ways that some politicians and many busy decision-takers might prefer. However, when it is performing its classic task of identifying similarities and differences between national educational policies and practices, comparative education upsets local definitions of what is taken as a problem and what is being taken as a solution. Like other modes of academic reflection on education, it is useful as a Cassandra voice: in casting doubt on conventional wisdom. But comparative education does not, and probably should not attempt to, speak in the voice of prophecy and advocacy. For all these reasons, this chapter does not embark upon an international search for examples of the best practice in initial teacher education and argue the case for their importation into England and Wales (or even more arrogantly into Britain).

The chapter works to a more limited set of objectives: to locate – against foreign experience – some of the policy tensions over initial teacher training in England and Wales during the last twenty years; and to contextualize this foreign educational experience as a guard against the trap of instant solutions. It is also worth noting that the foreign experience against which comparisons are made with ourselves keeps changing: there are fashions in comparisons.

For example, during the late sixties and seventies the tendency within American comparative education was to make comparisons between the USA and the USSR. In the 1980s, the Americans increasingly compared themselves with Japan. Similarly, the English comparative educationists during the sixties and early seventies displayed a strong interest in American educational reform, in areas such as secondary schooling, urban education, teacher education, multiculturalism, and higher education. From the mid-1980s, comparisons with Europe (although always a concern of such specialists as N Grant, W Halls, A Hearden, J Lauglo, V Mallinson and G Neave) increased in frequency, and were often offered by those with no particular expertise in European issues.

This chapter, in its comparisons, reflects that English ambivalence about whom we should compare ourselves with, as we measure our comparative progress. Many of the comparisons are drawn with northern and western Europe in the immediate present; but debates about initial teacher training are also located against American experience.

The themes of the comparisons are the impact, on initial training, of disputes about whom the teacher serves; what the teacher should know; and anxieties about contemporary crises in teacher education. In each case, the English situation will be contrasted with one or more situations overseas. The subtext of the comparisons is the 'progress' made by various countries in their teacher–education policies in relation to English debates.

Whom should the teacher serve?

Teaching as a profession

In this context, the grass-is-greener model has been the USA. In the mid-1960s when the English were debating the issue of improvement in the initial training of teachers, it was with the United States that a number of comparisons were drawn. The English were discussing among other things the upgrading of the qualifications of primary-school teachers and teachers who would work in the secondary-modern schools or with the younger children in comprehensive schools. It was in the USA that the process of institutional upgrading of teacher colleges and teacher qualifications had an early history of success. Particularly after the Second World War, the Americans gradually brought their single purpose, stand-alone, institutions of teacher education into colleges awarding bachelor degrees in a range of subjects, or into universities. By the late sixties, albeit with the usual regional variation which characterizes American education, tenure as a secondary-school teacher was partly dependent on being able to demonstrate that a masters degree in education was almost completed (at least in states with high expectations, like New York and California; in the southern states expectations were lower). Tenured employment in primary schools was dependent on possessing a bachelor's degree, normally a four-year qualification with a specialization in education in the last two years. The upshot was that the aspiration for an all-graduate profession by the late 1960s had been satisfied – although there was criticism about the 'mis-education of American teachers'(Conant, 1963; Koerner, 1963).

Just how close the American teacher was to being a member of a profession was debated in the literature (Lieberman, 1956). And this debate found reverberations in England: the idea that progress in English initial teacher training – in terms of institutional upgrading via the absorption of all teacher training into the universities, the lengthening of courses, the award of bachelor degrees – was to be measured against the American exemplar. Convergence to that ideal was desirable, and perhaps, at least in a 1960s view, possible.

Typically, the basis of the comparison and the measurement of convergence was one of the well-known models of a profession which were being created and utilized by sociologists (Jackson, 1970). Many of these models were 'ideal typical'(that is, following Max Weber, neither empirically typical, nor an aimed-at ideal. Rather the ideal-typical models were a synthesis and exaggeration of the characteristics of a particular social phenomenon. Against the models, actual practice might be measured). In terms of professions, these ideal-typical models stressed such characteristics of a profession as its provision of an essential public service, its esoteric knowledge, its control over the entry and exit procedures of its members, and the altruism of professions confirmed by clear codes of ethical practice. There are some disadvantages to the technique (Hoyle, 1980).

In particular, ideal-typical models which concentrate on defining what a profession *is*, tend to conceal the social processes by which professions have been created. Models of the internal characteristics of a profession conceal the historical theme of how abstract knowledge was turned into economic and social power in the market place by an increasingly organized oligarchy, with the acquiesence of the state (Larson, 1977). Secondly, models which concentrate on the internal characteristics of a profession tend to underestimate the importance of the role of the state itself, as a potential actor in education and teacher education.

Thus, among the comparativists at least, and perhaps among educationists, there developed an underestimation of the amount of insulation and de facto delegation which the English system of teacher training had developed. That is, in England (and in Australia, Canada and the USA) the institutions of higher education, particularly the universities, had begun to determine the details of teacher training. What the ahistorical nature of the ideal-typical modelling permitted was an underestimation of the (English) state's earlier detailed control over teacher education, and a reduction of the problem of state influence to managerial issues such as how to increase the supply of teachers.

However, in both the USA from the early 1970s and in England from the late 1970s, the level of political interest and intervention in education and teacher education increased.

In the United States, the movement took the form of anxiety about returns, from the educational system, for each tax-dollar spent. Among the reactions were a renewed emphasis on the testing of pupil achievement in the schools, and competency-based teacher-education schemes to guarantee minimum levels of teacher performance. By the late 1970s in the USA, more than half the states (whose legal responsibility it is to provide education) had established competency-based teacher education training programmes (Burton, 1977). These programmes affected very directly those institutions (including the universities) which provided initial teacher training. Changes had to be made in patterns of initial teacher training to fit state specifications.

Without state approval, graduates of institutions would not have their academic qualifications, and training in education, turned into licences to teach.

In England, the movement took the form of anxiety about whether the English educational system was assisting in the creation of a wealth-generating and entrepreneurial society in comparison with our competitors (like Japan and Western Germany). The view was pressed hard by several politicians and a number of pressure groups, that we were failing in that competition, and that one of the contributory factors was the quality of teachers and the way they were trained.

There was increasing intervention by the state in the details (Department of Educational Science, 1983a) of teacher training from 1983 and 1984 through the Advisory Committee on the Supply and Education of Teachers and Circular 3/84 (Gosden, 1989; Department of Educational Science, 1984). Subsequently, mechanisms – notably the use of Her Majesty's Inspectors – were established to keep under review programmes of teacher training, which were to be reformed in accordance with criteria which the Council for the Accreditation of Teacher Education (CATE) was asked to operationalize.

In other words the actual criteria used for accrediting institutions of teacher training were altered (in practice in England and in law and in practice in the United States). The English institutions of teacher training, including the universities, began the reform of their programmes, so that their graduates might continue to turn their academic qualifications and training in education into licences to teach.

In contrast, within many countries of continental Europe, teachers are state employees in the formal sense: they are civil servants. This is the case, with minor variations in precise legal status in Belgium, Denmark, France, the Federal Republic of Germany and Luxembourg. However, this has by no means removed anxieties about professional status, nor has it insulated teachers from state action designed to upgrade teacher qualifications.

The historic dual-track division in European teacher education (between those educated in the university and those who were educated in other institutions, often upper secondary schools) came under severe pressure with the movement towards a common lower secondary school. Then, somewhat as in England with the grammar-school teachers and the primary-school teachers, the discrepancy of statuses within the 'profession' became the more visible. Within the teaching force, in France and Germany to take two extreme examples, there was the sharpest of demarcation between those teachers in the *lycées* and the *Gymnasien* who belonged to the *Société des Agrégés* and the *Philologenverband*, and primary-school teachers (Mallinson, 1980; Judge, 1988). Efforts since the mid-1960s, as in England, have been made to upgrade the formal qualifications of primary and lower-secondary-school teachers. By the mid-1980s, the training of primary-school teachers had lengthened to three or four years, after the completion of general secondary education (eg in Belgium, France, and Luxembourg). And in most countries of north west Europe, teacher education had been relocated within higher education – sometimes universities (eg the Republic of Ireland), sometimes non-university institutions within higher education (eg Denmark, the Federal Republic of Germany, and the Netherlands).

Thus initial teacher education has been and is being reformed by state action in England, the USA and in continental Europe. The reform of teacher education and of training, by state agencies, has re-clarified that teachers are national (or regional) state employees. In present political climates – in most of continental Europe, England and the United States – it seems very unlikely that teachers could turn themselves into a high-status traditional profession modelled on the example of occupational groups such as lawyers and doctors. Indeed, at the present moment, such oligarchies of expertise are under attack (eg in England), in the name of improving competition and the quality of service to the consumer.

Teachers and the community

Teachers not only serve a national community on terms acceptable to the state (a proposition very crisply expressed after a revolution or in the 'demilitarization' of teachers in the occupied countries after the Second World War), they also serve a local community. How teachers do this, and how they are prepared in initial training to perceive the local community varies considerably in comparative perspective. English schools have traditionally been insulated from the surrounding local community. In comparative terms this was true of all English schools; but in the English context, it was particularly true of the grammar and public schools. The teaching there provided an avenue for local and national economic and social mobility. As well as preparing children for white collar local jobs, the academic and social culture of many of the grammar schools and perhaps most of the public schools anticipated some of the academic and social culture of the London–Oxford–Cambridge metropolitan triangle of universities.

The relationship of the public school to the local community was often that of sharp insulation. The relationship of the grammar school and the grammar-school teacher to the local community was rather ambivalent. The teacher was simultaneously a member of the community (often a politically active member), but also one who served it through representing the academic values and the social culture of a non-local world (Ree, 1956; Davies, 1965; Stevens, 1960). Thus the role of the grammar-school teacher was fundamentally legitimated by the values of the university and the symbol of the BA or the MA which the teachers normally carried from that university system; and by the teacher's importance in increasing, on the basis of academic performance, individuals' opportunities to enter higher education.

The relationship of the American schoolteacher to his or her community, to the national academic community and to the higher-education system, has different traditions (Waller, 1965). The tradition interprets the schoolteacher as the servant of the local community, the school as locally financed, and the school and classroom as more or less permanently open to parental inspection. The schoolteacher ought, both in details of personal behaviour and in pedagogy, to confirm the values of the local community. Teaching things which are wrong according to the values of the local community (for example, teaching Darwinian versions of evolution, or criticizing the Vietnam war too early, are among the most publicized cases) may bring censure or dismissal.

The traditional relationship in the USA of secondary schools and secondary-school teachers to the national academic community and the higher-education system was also different. In the United States, the values of an academic tradition had been weakened, at the secondary-school level, with the decline of the nineteenth-century academy and the increasing stress upon the common school. Certainly from the start of this century, the schools did far more than concentrate on their linkages with higher education (Tyack, 1974). They prepared students for work, often in the local community, incorporating industrial arts and home economics into the curriculum; through social studies, the schools offered an understanding of American democracy at local and national levels; and through an increasing range of non-academic courses they provided useful skills for social living (of which the contemporary variants are courses like driving education and anti-drug education programmes). Thus the culture of the American high school is less influenced than the traditional schools systems of Europe by versions of a university academic culture.

Currently, access to higher education is partly through school grades and general educational record; but also through standardized tests which are not directly set by the universities. Relatively little, then, insulates the schools and the teachers from local community pressures, expressed directly by parents or through the local school boards and the local school superintendent.

Of course, with the emergence, especially at the lower-secondary level, of the comprehensive school model in much of Europe, there has been some convergence of institutional patterns. Furthermore, the English tradition of carefully separating schools from direct concerns

world of work has been affected by innovations (such as
)uth unemployment, and a concomitant stress on how young
to grasp – or even to create – local employment opportunities.
, , efforts have been made over the last twenty years to extend
the examination and qualification system to include pupils other than
those who are seeking access to higher education.

Nevertheless, the elements of convergence should not be exaggerated.
It is not being suggested here that English teachers are being trained for
American style community – school relations.

Indeed, there are some unique oddities in current English developments, perhaps because of the tension between certain left-wing local
authorities and the current Conservative central government. An
expectation has been established, through Circular 3/84, that teachers
in training will develop

> a basic understanding of the type of society in which their pupils are
> growing up, with its cultural and racial mix, and of the relationships
> between the adult world and what is taught in schools, in particular,
> ways in which pupils can be helped to acquire an understanding of
> the values of a free society and its economic and other foundations
> (DES, 1984, p 26).

If we ignore for a moment the reference to a cultural and racial mix,
the proposition can be read in a variety of ways. At one level it merely
captures the rhetoric of several federal-level reports in the USA after
1945, when free societies had to be defended in a Cold-War world. At
another level, it can be interpreted as stressing that an enterprise culture
should be encouraged in the schools, by teachers trained in fresh ways
and in a fresh spirit.

Here, however, the point which is most relevant for the analysis is
that the circular is suggesting that teachers transmit a national culture
to their pupils. The change is from the transmission of a disciplines-
based academic culture, in the grammar school or public school, to the
transmission of an understanding of the problems of the adult world and
the values appropriate to function within it. What remains the same is
that the teacher carries responsibilities to the nation, defined as it were
from London. Certain values are to be taken into local communities.
The teacher, through improved initial-training programmes, will be
better equipped to handle the task; but the teacher is an active agent
in transmitting values external to the local community rather than a
reflector of local assumptions.

The argument being developed at this point is also relevant in the area
of multicultural education. Being trained for multicultural education
during initial training is now – following the Swann Report, the
Rampton Committee and the DES Command Paper, *Better Schools* –

a national expectation. But the expectation is framed in a rejection of assimilation policies, and stresses the multicultural and pluralist nature of contemporary Britain. This message, encouraged as it were from London, must be transmitted in a context of some local communities preferring assimilation as a social and educational policy. Again, English teachers and presumably newly recruited ethnic-minority teachers are expected not to be over-responsive to the values of local communities. This is different from American and some Canadian experience, where local pressures have been very important. In Atlanta, in Boston, in New York, and in Quebec City, for example legislation to control local variation has been introduced at the national level with the intention of safeguarding the cultural heritage of children, where necessary offering bilingual and bicultural instruction.

In addition to this question of how the teacher is being introduced to the community, there is a further puzzle in English education currently about how the community is being introduced into the school. The stress would seem to be on parents as consumers of education, who on market principles will increasingly be able to choose good schools for their children: to vote, as it were, with their children's feet. This is a very limited linkage of schools with their local communities. American parents are consumers of education too, and often choose their place of residence in relation to the availability of good schools. But thereafter there is considerable permeability (over curriculum, styles of pedagagy for example) between community members and the local schools (Beattie, 1985).

The previous discussion has begun to open up the question of what teachers should learn in their initial training. It is now useful to turn directly to that issue and locate it in comparative context.

What should teachers know?

Knowledge of academic subjects and knowledge of education

In the United States, as already indicated, there was a major debate in the mid-1960s over whether teachers had sufficient knowledge of the academic subjects they were to teach.

The academic traditions of the English and European secondary-school systems, and the fact that the teachers within the prestige academic secondary schools were educated in universities, meant that the English and European debate has focused on upgrading the primary-school teacher's qualifications, rather than worrying a great deal about the academic qualifications of the secondary and upper-secondary teacher.

The reforms in continental Europe as in England have tended to include a stress upon a command of subjects such as language and mathematics for all teachers, including primary teachers (eg Belgium and the Netherlands). Sometimes, this is combined with an emphasis on preparing teachers to teach all subjects at primary level (eg the Netherlands and the Federal Republic of Germany).

Conversely, for teachers in secondary schools, the stress has increasingly moved toward linking initial teacher education more closely to the schools (eg France, the Federal Republic of Germany, the Netherlands and England). Coupled with this has been an increase in the amount of time given to *how* to teach, for example in Belgium, Italy and the Netherlands. This concern with how to teach has taken different definitions in mainland Europe, and in England and the USA. In Europe, the specificities of how to teach are embedded within and, in principle, are deducible from, a general theory of instruction and learning taught to teachers in training under the name of didactics. In England, there has developed greater and greater expertise on how to teach particular subjects, without a parallel development of a general theory of teaching and learning.

These two particular issues (linking training with schools, and deciding how to teach teachers how to teach) are part of a broader issue: the question of what teachers need to know, not only about schooling and teaching but also education, especially when teacher training is tightly linked to schools and when there is no widely accepted theory of teaching (Simon, 1981).

In answering this question, the English tradition is clear. Up to the middle of the 1970s in both university and colleges of education, the normal mix was knowledge of the 'foundations of education' (philosophy, sociology, psychology, though these might often be combined with studies of the history of education or the administration of education or comparative education) (Tibble, 1966) in combination with exposure to practical teaching, and seminars, workshops and lectures on how to teach.

England is among those countries which have recently begun to link teacher education more tightly to schools, partly as a result of the CATE criteria. Whether the CATE criteria have been overinterpreted or not, the consequences have been a less formal and structured introduction to the foundation areas in teacher training. The practical results have been an increase in the number of courses which are seen as directly related to school practice, such as 'education and the computer', 'schooling and museums', and 'the use of photography' as a teaching aid and technique in schools.

This pattern of change has had the virtue of increasing the teacher's range of expertise which may be applied practically in the schools. It has had the disadvantage of separating teachers, in their initial training, from a systematic introduction to those forms of knowledge which encourage reflection of the broader aspects of the teacher's role and the social, political and economic significance of education.

The stress on linking teacher education more closely with the schools has one similarity with the competency-based teacher-education movement in the United States: what the extreme version of both the English and the American models raises, is the possibility of abolishing teacher education in institutions outside of the schools altogether. Clearly, if existing teacher behaviour and craftsmanship is the main correct measure of a competent teacher, then the best place to learn these competencies is in the classroom. Competency-based teacher education was a model based on a careful analysis of what teachers in classrooms do, and how this knowledge could be broken down into manageable modules. Students would either demonstrate competency in those behaviours, or, if they could not do so, they would take the relevant competency module. The basic focus of those programmes was on teacher behaviour – many of the programmes were based in behaviourist psychology (Magoon, 1976) – and the model of knowledge which emerged distanced initial teacher education from, among other things, some of the classical writers on education, such as Plato, Rousseau, Durkheim and Max Weber.

In the English context this sounds, a priori, rather uncivilized; and no doubt blame may be, and probably is being, put upon a cast of villains – whether 'the government', the DES, HMI, CATE or the London Institute of Education. However, in a comparative perspective, it seems unwise to simplify the agencies and causes. Underestimated in such perceptions of the shift away from the foundation subjects, in initial and more advanced training, is the issue of how the demarcations of content in educational studies are influenced by the economic division of labour in education.

In the United States, the division of educational studies into separate branches is strongly linked with opportunities for employment in education. Thus, for example, department of higher education within American schools of education, as well as awarding PhDs, prepare their successful graduates for jobs in the administration of higher education. Departments of instruction and curriculum in the USA prepare not only teachers in initial training for work in the schools, but also train curriculum advisers for employment with city-level or rural-area boards of education. In a similar fashion in England, the survival of the foundation of education areas in initial teacher training was linked with the impact of the universities, through the Area Training Organizations, on the definition and examination of courses in the colleges; and with the education and academic certification of lecturers (at Advanced

Diploma and MA levels) to teach foundation areas in those colleges. The relative decline of the foundation areas is linked to the lack of major career opportunities (as a result of the closure of many colleges of education in the seventies) for those who graduate with specialist degrees in philosophy of education, sociology of education and so on. New attitudes have emerged about what is relevant knowledge for the young teacher; and within in-service training, new patterns of financing and control, and the demand for very short and practical courses by local education authorities (who pay), have compounded the speed of change.

The consequence has been a growth in the specific expertise and classroom applicability of the knowledge which teachers gain in initial training. Many new skills and many particular bits of expertise seem to be called for to solve a range of problems. Some of these problems, for example the demands of multiculturalism, arise from the changing nature of English society. Some arise from growth in the size of schools – management skills have become essential. And some problems have arisen at the intersection of schools with large bureaucracies of intervention: the intrusion into the schools of a flurry of local and national memoranda. New expertise is being called for.

The consequence has been that teachers are increasingly treated as employees, and as employees of large bureaucracies. Following management principles, they must possess measureable skills, have job descriptions, and be upgradable. They must be experts, in the Max Weber sense. The older versions of the (Weberian idea of the) cultivated teacher are disappearing. And, in England, a new science of pedagogy has not been invented.

Pedagogy and expertise

There has been considerable discussion about the impact of the National Curriculum. That need not be re-rehearsed here. But what is worth emphasizing is that the English are on the point not only of diminishing the control by teachers over the timing and pacing of their work (as well as diminishing the influence of teachers over their material conditions of work and pay) but also on the point of stabilizing pedagogy – the principles and practice of teaching – as a set of separated expertises, within institutions which are increasingly responsive to market forces and which are increasingly judged in terms of concepts of 'management' and 'efficiency'. The processes of negotiating this position have included strong attacks by major government figures on the probable incompetence of some teachers; and the context of response has included, within a climate of enterprise and profit, the emergence of teaching as a less and less attractive occupation to many of those formally qualified to enter teacher-education courses.

These developments have extremely strong parallels with an early moment in American educational history. During that period, the American school administrator emerged as a separate 'profession' and the language of business began to dominate the perspectives through which schools were viewed. The American teacher became an administered teacher; the most able teachers moved into administration; and school systems, characterized by city-wide syllabuses, close testing and monitoring, tried to become teacher-proof. It is doubtful if US education has ever quite recovered from that burst of efficiency (Callahan, 1962). In comparative perspective, many US schools are top-heavy with management; teachers begin to question early in their careers how they can get out of the classroom; there is very frequent classroom-level testing of children; and a sense of the vision and excitement of teaching and learning has tended to disappear.

The English have moved closer to the businesslike – in both senses of the word – model of American schooling. They have narrowed their definitions of what a competent teacher is. The English will shortly have lots more information about the effects of their schooling system – which no doubt will permit it to be managed (by professionals) and consumed (by parents and children) even more efficiently.

But to have come closer to being businesslike is not necessarily a victory, or a definition of educational progress, or a definition of comparative progress.

Much depends on what has been and is being lost. Among the things which are being lost, at the moment at least, is the willingness of young people to take up the work of being a teacher. Sooner or later, the national government and our society will have to pay a price for that.

Chapter 4

Thinking and Research on Teacher Education

Norman Graves

Personal motivation

I have spent much of my working life at the 'sharp end' of teacher education, namely, teaching secondary PGCE students how to get pupils and students to learn a particular subject area. What seemed to matter was helping the students to manage 30 or more pupils, to learn how to structure a lesson or teaching unit so that pupils would be motivated and would learn something worthwhile, to learn how to evaluate what the pupils had themselves learned, and to learn how to evaluate their own work as teachers. I had always been conscious that such apparently straightforward tasks were in practice complicated in part because a good deal of thinking was required (if only to be clear about what was worthwhile) and by the multiplicity of skills (social and managerial) that students had to learn. The courses for which I was responsible, at both the PGCE and MA level, evolved in the light of our experience of them as tutors and in the light of the evaluation we received from students. Thus when my responsibilities changed from being responsible for one subject department to that of being in charge of a whole PGCE course, it was clear to me that the 'method course' I now left to someone else, was a very different course (and in my view a better one), from the one I inherited.

However, when I was given ultimate responsibility for the whole PGCE course, I was faced with proposals to change the structure of the course; proposals made by a working party of which I had not been a member and to whose thinking I had not been privy. It was necessary for me to examine what general developments had occurred in teacher education as a whole, and what models of teacher training were now informing practice. What follows is thus an exploration of thinking and research which has occurred since the early seventies, concentrating mainly on the 1980s. Although I will focus on the United Kingdom, some of the ideas which have influenced teacher education have their origins in North America and these will be considered.

Background

Professor Wragg, in his inimitable style, stated in 1984 that when he first entered teacher training in the mid–1960s, students were given courses of lectures in the history, philosophy, psychology and sociology of education, and this he argued was equivalent to giving

> trainee surgeons a course of lectures on the history, philosophy and mechanics of surgery, and then turning them loose in the operating theatre, each twirling a scalpel, hoping the lectures would inform their incisions (Wragg, 1984).

He was, of course, exaggerating to make a point, since he used himself to teach a course on how to teach a modern foreign language (German in his case) to his students at Exeter University. But his point was, and many students in teacher education agreed with him, that the immediate relevance of the courses in the so-called foundation disciplines of education was not always clearly related to the tasks the trainee teachers had to undertake during their teaching practice. My own experience parallels Professor Wragg's, though at the Institute of Education at the University of London, the foundations-of-education courses were at that time taught by distinguished professors such as Richard Peters for philosophy of education, Philip Vernon for psychology of education and Basil Bernstein for sociology of education; such courses could not be lightly dismissed. The question which needs to be posed is what model of teacher education underlay courses consisting mainly of three elements: methods of teaching, foundation courses, and teaching practice?

Professor Wragg answered that question in a book published in 1974 in which he traces the model to that put forward as far back as 1907 by a 'Committee of Seventeen' of the National Education Association in the USA when it was examining teacher training for secondary schools (Wragg, 1974). The underlying assumptions behind such a programme of teacher education expected a future member of the teaching profession to know:

- how education had changed over time (history of education);
- how the workings of the mind might affect the process of teaching (psychology of education);
- what values inform the ends toward which the education process was working (philosophy of education);

- what teaching techniques are generally applicable and which are specific to a particular subject (methods of teaching);
- how schools and the education system work (the organization and management of schools and school systems);
- how pupils might be kept healthy (hygiene).

Inevitably, over time, the nature of these courses was modified and some acquired new titles, such as health education instead of hygiene. Perhaps the most significant change, introduced in the 1960s by Richard Peters, was to make the foundations-of-education courses much more academically rigorous than they had been in the past. The argument behind this move was that in a university one could not condone courses in philosophy, psychology and sociology which were in certain respects at an intellectually lower level than parallel courses in departments of philosophy, psychology or sociology elsewhere in the university – though it was understood they would not necessarily cover the same ground.

While it is easy to understand why the suggestions of the 'Committee of Seventeen' were readily accepted and spread to the United Kingdom, it is also plain with hindsight that the kind of propositional knowledge offered in the foundation disciplines was not immediately usable in the process of learning to manage a class or teach how to solve a problem in mathematics or physics. Indeed the students on teacher-education courses, most of whom had a starkly instrumental view of what such a course should provide, were not slow in making their feelings known. On the whole, students would readily accept the need for teaching method courses and teaching practice, but were at best ambivalent about foundations-of-education courses, though some conceded that these could be intellectually stimulating and interesting.

John Wilson, an Oxford philosopher, wrote a thoughtful book on *Educational Theory and the Preparation of Teachers* in 1975 (Wilson, 1975). The main thrust of his thesis was to explicate the concept of education and in the light of this to propose that teacher preparation should ensure that prospective teachers have:

- a professional attitude, ie that they understand what rationality and learning are about and why they are important;
- knowledge of a conceptual and factual nature about what is to be taught, ie the subject matter;
- personal knowledge, ie knowledge about people, their intentions, emotions;
- know-how, ie non-propositional knowledge: the skills and competencies necessary to carry the job of managing pupils;
- the necessary motivation to carry out the job of teaching.

He also wrote on many other aspects of teacher education, but his whole emphasis was on the sorting-out of ideas and practices and the reinforcement of the notion that practice could lead nowhere without a solid underpinning of theoretical knowledge. He had less to say about how the 'know-how', which he recognized as an essential element of teacher education, could be imparted.

It is here that we need to go back to the USA and look at the ideas of Donald Schön.

Donald Schön and the reflective practitioner

Donald Schön was academically educated in philosophy at Yale and Harvard universities but became professionally involved in the business world as an industrial and social consultant. During his time as a consultant he became interested in the problem of change and the need for individuals and societies to form organisms and organizations that learn how to adapt. His ideas on this were broadcast as the Reith Lectures on the BBC in 1970 and published by Temple-Smith in 1971 (Schön, 1971). One striking feature of his analysis of change is the notion of dynamic conservatism, namely the tendency for individuals and organizations to resist change vigorously by developing structures or mechanisms which make change difficult. In academic life the departmental structures which have developed over time provide a stable state for the members; changes which threaten this state are resisted strongly. Thus interdepartmental courses are not popular because they threaten the autonomy of each department. In my own experience, trying to get staff to participate in courses which lie outside the remit of their own departments meets with resistance on the grounds that they are too busy teaching on other courses or that they have been given extra administrative duties which would prevent them teaching and so on. Clearly such dynamic conservatism applies to courses of teacher education as well as to others.

Schön's argument in *Beyond the Stable State* is that, gradually, organizations need to become learning systems and that the process is helped if change is not attempted in a large organization by imposing it from the centre to the periphery. Rather, is it easier and produces less opposition if change is allowed to take place in the peripheral areas of an organization and gradually communicate itself throughout the corporate body. An example of this is the idea of what is now known as school-based work (or serial practice) which started in one department at the Institute of Education and then gradually spread to other departments, so that by the time it became the Institute's policy, many departments were already using it.

Schön then became interested in the way people in the professions were educated, partly arising out of his previous work as a consultant and partly as a result of his appointment to the chair of urban studies and education at the Massachusetts Institute of Technology (MIT). In fact, some of his thinking concerning reflection-in-action can be seen in embryonic form in *Beyond the Stable State*, where he discourses on the practical difficulties of implementing what he calls 'the national/experimental model of public learning'. The main trigger which led to his developing his thesis of the reflective practitioner was his being invited to take part in a study of architectural education at MIT. This resulted in the publication of *The Reflective Practitioner* in 1983, in which he expounded his ideas on what he calls a new epistemology of practice. Subsequently, in 1987, he expounded on the kind of education which would be appropriate for professional practice, in *Educating the Reflective Practitioner*.

To make sense of proposals for professional education, it is important to understand what Schön means by professional knowledge. First, his analysis is not limited to any one profession; indeed he uses examples from many professions – architecture, engineering, music-making, psychiatry and teaching. Secondly, he sees as inherent in the practice of competent professionals what he calls a 'core of artistry'. Artistry for him

> is an exercise in intelligence, a kind of knowing, though different in crucial aspects from our standard model of professional knowledge. It is not inherently mysterious; it is rigorous in its own terms; and we can learn a great deal about it – within what limits, we should treat as an open question – by carefully studying the performance of unusually competent performers (Schön, 1987).

Such practitioners 'know-in-action': they are able to deal with a problem by immediate, apparently non-logical, processes. Examples would be the medical practitioner who can recognize a disease as soon as a patient walks into the surgery; the architect who can see a solution to the problem of fitting a building to an unpromising site; the teacher who sees where the pupil's thinking has gone wrong in attempting to solve a mathematical problem. However, these professionals did not get to their present state of expertise or artistry by magic; they got there, states Schön, by reflection-in-action.

Essentially, this is a process of learning from the results of one's actions. It is more than a pure trial-and-error process, since it involves reflecting on unsuccessful actions (actions which did not produce the desired result) and evolving more appropriate ones. It involves a kind of continuing adjustment to feedback resulting from action. Sometimes this is continuous and rapid, as when a group of jazz musicians are improvising, or when a teacher is dealing with a class-management problem; sometimes it may be slower, as when a teacher, having attempted to teach the concept of relative humidity in an abstract way and failed, needs to reflect on why s/he has failed and in what way the concept could be presented in a more concrete manner. The point that I interpret Schön to be making is that one can develop in students a capability for reflection-in-action, but one cannot tell a student, for example, that if s/he teaches relative humidity in a certain way, one can guarantee that the pupils will learn the concept. In other words, technical rationality does not always work.

This view of professional knowledge as artistry (or know-how or expertise) involves a shift from an objectivist to a constructivist view of practice. If such a shift occurs, then critically important terms such as truth and effectiveness become problematic. They cannot be applied to every situation, they are only relevant to the particular context or 'frame' being considered. The problem for those who educate for the professions is that an objectivist epistemology of practice has been at the heart of university thinking since the late nineteenth century. Practice is seen as the result of instrumental problem-solving and becomes professional practice when it is based on systematic and preferably scientific knowledge. Hence the past insistence that university courses of teacher education should be based on what Schön calls *technical rationality* – in this case philosophy, psychology and sociology – whilst those dealing with the 'artistry' of teaching (the methods lecturers) were looked upon as second class (Patrick, 1986). This creates the dilemma of universities asking for rigour while the students and practitioners ask for relevance.

What kind of professional education might be appropriate to an epistemology of practice based on *reflection-in-action*? According to Schön, such professional education must bring 'learning by doing' into the core of the curriculum. In terms of teacher education, this means that teaching practice (in whatever form) should be the central aspect of the course from which students can learn by reflection-in-action, aided by competent practitioners (the teachers in schools and lecturers concerned with professional practice). If that is to happen, then those who coach or counsel in what Schön calls a 'reflective practicum' must be valued by the institutions employing them, that is they should be considered on equal terms in the pay and promotion stakes, with those involved in the traditional disciplines. However, though those concerned with the 'reflective practicum' will develop an ethos and terminology of their own, they need to keep in touch both with the world of practice (the schools) and the world of science and scholarship, so that reflective practice is informed from these two sources. Those of us who have been concerned with methods of teaching and supervising teaching practice have been conscious for a long time of the need to keep in balance these two sources of wisdom on teaching. Lastly, Schön warns that learning from reflective practice is not a rapid process, but one which takes time.

Parallel developments in thinking and research about teacher education

Whether or not Schön was the first to use the term 'reflective practitioner',* there is little doubt that since the publication of his book with that title, the idea has caught on. Joan Soloman (1987) makes direct reference to Schön in an article which argues that neither the theory-led nor the apprenticeship model of teacher education are by themselves adequate for the task of the professional preparation of teachers. As Soloman has it:

- the practitioner's craft knowledge needs to be made articulate and communicated to students;
- students need to develop the life-long habit of reflection in action and to recognize that the knowledge obtained is situationally dependent;
- such knowledge can be enhanced by inputs from appropriate disciplines; and
- reflection also involves a temporary withdrawal from the 'hurly-burly' classroom practice.

Similarly, Handal and Lauris (1987) devote a short book to showing how teaching-practice supervisors may undertake counselling to enable student teachers to develop into reflective practitioners; this seems to be clearly inspired by Schön's ideas. In essence, they ask students, in reflecting on what they have done in classrooms, to examine the assumptions they have made about their pupils and the knowledge they attempted to teach; to analyse what happened in the classroom; and to examine what criteria of learning success they have and how valid these criteria are. They want students to realize that 'good teaching' is not describable independently of contextual factors and ultimate aims and that the same aims may be reached by a number of different routes.

There is further explicit reference to Schön ideas in a book edited

*Elliot Eisner hinted at a similar view of teaching in his 1979 book *The Educational Imagination*

by John Smyth (1987) which contains 16 chapters written mostly by American authors on '*Educating Teachers: Changing the Nature of Pedagogical Knowledge*'. The book is divided into three sections. The first deals with pedagogical knowledge, the second with pedagogical contexts and the third with pedagogical action. The book attempts to carry the debate further, though since it consists of the thoughts of 16 individuals with different experiences and backgrounds, it is difficult to discern firm trends, save the determination to develop the work of teachers along reflective-practitioner lines.

A recent book which purports to be in part inspired by Schön's work is Della Fish's '*Learning through Practice in Initial Teacher Training*' (1989), more closely geared to the British situation than Smyth's can be. Although it makes certain proposals for professional courses of initial training, I should like to leave these to one side for the moment to consider developments which do not apparently stem directly from Schön's ideas.

One strand of thinking about teacher education is what I will call the humanistic strand. It stems from the alternative views of schooling and education made popular by such writers as Illich, Freire and Milanesi in the 1960s and early 1970s, though I am not implying that these writers had only one view of alternative schooling. A good example of the humanistic attitude to teacher education is given in Gwyneth Dow's book '*Learning to Teach, Teaching to Learn*' (1979). Dow gives an almost 'blow-by-blow' account of an 'alternative' course in teacher training for graduates at the University of Melbourne in Australia, which started in 1973. It is difficult to argue that the course was based on any one particular model of teacher training, though one structural feature is clear: it was centred around the 'methods-of-teaching' seminars. Since the course was concerned with secondary students who were required in schools to teach two subjects, each student attended two methods-of-teaching seminars, for example the teaching of English and the teaching of history. The rationale behind this was that students were to be spending much of their time teaching particular subjects in schools, and therefore their prime concern was with learning how to teach these subjects as well as possible. Other issues in education would arise naturally out of this activity: why they should teach certain things (aims in education), how they should teach (what would motivate pupils, what would stretch them intellectually, how to manage their classes), what bias might arise in relation to ethnic groups, gender, and so on. However, what leads me to describe the approach as humanistic is not the structure of the course but the emphasis which is placed on personal relationships and on introspection. Students are asked to record their feelings in diaries and to analyse how they came to terms with the ways in which their own personalities were not always in harmony with the teaching personalities they adopted or the teaching styles they used. Similarly they were asked to look into their relationships with the pupils they taught and to develop affective but controlled bonds with them. Further, the students were asked to assess themselves and agree with tutors whether they ought to pass or fail their teaching practice. Thus the tenor of this alternative course was on feelings and emotions and the development of warm relationships in the educational process. It could be argued that this was a form of reflection on practice, though in my interpretation it is a different form of reflection from that preconized later by Schön.

As might be expected, not all students (or tutors) were entirely happy with this kind of course. In fact Gwyneth Dow herself wonders whether such a course may be suitable for radical students only. She also raises the question of the function of schoolteachers in the training process. She sees teacher education as a process needing a partnership between teachers, lecturers and students, but this seems to arise out of pragmatic considerations rather than as an integral part of the alternative course. There is no clear model of this partnership which integrates it with the alternative course as described. Nevertheless, the word partnership in the training of teachers struck a chord among other innovators, and the term was to become the leitmotif of new teacher-education schemes.

Gwyneth Dow's alternative course was an attempt at one form of empirical research into teacher education. In England and Wales, there occurred a number of projects whose purpose was to examine teacher education in an empirical manner. Wragg's comments about courses based on the disciplines of education (quoted at the beginning of this chapter) were made in the context of one such project, The Teacher Education Project, which began in 1976 and lasted until 1981. It was directed by Professor Wragg, financed by the Department of Education and Science (DES) and based on the universities of Nottingham and Leicester. As was implied by Wragg's comments, he felt that not enough attention had been given in the past to developing the teaching skills of student teachers. He did not wish, however, to go down the line followed in certain American states, whereby long lists of so-called 'competencies' were produced, a high percentage of which teachers were expected to demonstrate their capacity to perform satisfactorily. The project team decided to concentrate their attention on class management, mixed-ability teaching, questioning and explaining. There was no intention to produce a course, but 'rather to devise teaching materials and ways of working which might help shift the balance of teacher-training courses more in the direction of the development of professional skills . . .' (Wragg 1984). The method adopted was to observe over 1,000 lessons given by students and teachers and distil from this evidence – and from other sources – procedures which in published form would help both students and practising teachers. These were mainly published in the *FOCUS Workbooks* by Macmillan, each workbook having been tested in two trial versions.

Essentially, the approach was pragmatic: what are the main problems that students face when they begin teaching? How do competent teachers deal with these problems? How can students adapt their behaviour to solve those problems for themselves? Although Wragg did not set out to produce a course, he nevertheless has a theoretical position about training teachers. He asserts that an inductive approach in which experience precedes any theorizing about practice is a sensible way to proceed, since not only do some theoretical positions make more sense when seen in the contexts of experience, but experience provides a basis for being critical of theory. In this he is not poles apart from Schön's reflective practitioner. He does recognize that one danger in this approach is the possibility that students might be inducted into a practice which extolled current methods and did not sufficiently look forward to the development of practice.

Another expert who wrote extensively in the 1970s and 1980s on teacher education is Edgar Stones. Although he stresses particularly what he calls psychopedagogy (Stones 1978), I understand him to mean something similar to Wragg's thoughts about the need to impart teaching skills. He emphasizes enquiry and learning on the part of the student:

> 'Student teachers' learning will equip them to solve pedagogical problems in a variety of teaching situations through a grasp of some general principles of teaching that transcend the teaching of specific subjects to specific groups of pupils. Supervisors themselves will also be involved, perhaps in a different way, but subject to the same learning processes' (Stones, 1984).

Stones aims to make the student autonomous, able to solve pedagogical problems by him or herself, but with the help of principles which he believes 'are most likely to be found in the literature on psychology and human learning.' By these principles he implies the principles of problem-solving, of concept-learning, of the development of motor skills, of human motivation, particularly when these principles are applied to a real-life situation. Thus he sees student and tutor exploring a teaching experience together in the light of such psychological principles – and learning from the experience.

We have here something different, though not completely divorced from, the concept of 'artistry' in professional performance as expounded by Schön. Stones wants a reflective practitioner (though he does not use the term), but one who is applying psychological theory in practice, granted the psychological principles have been acquired in a practical situation through enquiry learning. He also stresses the need for a symbiotic relationship between specialist subject knowledge and pedagogical theory, by which I understand him to mean that *how* something is taught is as much a function of *what* is to be taught as of pedagogical principles. To revert to my earlier example of relative humidity, since this is a human-created idea (a concept by definition according to Gagné) it is not something one can acquire entirely by observation or discovery, and so some exposition is necessary. This does not prevent reference being made to the experience of humid or dry air, but such experience cannot by itself teach the concept of relative humidity.

One area where Stones and Schön came very close to one another is in the learning that comes from observing what Schön has called an 'exceptionally competent practitioner'. Stones argues that, though much emphasis has been placed in the last ten years or so on the primacy and quantity of practice in a teacher-education course, little has been said about the quality of that practice. Yet many students do not necessarily observe 'exceptionally competent practitioners', so Stones must have doubts about the nature of that learning process, unless it is bolstered up by other experiences.

Although Stones draws from his own experience in teacher education he was not directly involved in a large-scale experimental teacher-education project. There were in England and Wales three further such projects which paralleled that directed by Wragg. One is the IT-INSET project directed by Patricia Ashton, based first on the Open University and later on Leicester University, and financed by the DES from 1978 to 1987. It thus overlapped with the Teacher Education Project. To quote Ashton, the IT-INSET view of teacher education

> argues that continuous improvement depends upon the quality of teachers' theorizing about learning and teaching. Constructive theorizing develops through skilled evaluation of learning and professional collaboration. It is suggested that these processes should pervade initial and in-service training and that teacher education is enriched when students, teachers and tutors teach, evaluate and theorize in classrooms together. IT-INSET thus represents both a philosophy of teacher education and a school-based programme of collaborative learning (Ashton et al, 1989).

Its essential practice is that a basic 'learning unit' of six students, one teacher and one tutor spend one half day or a whole day per week in a school, where they work together to plan, execute and discuss the learning which may or may not have taken place. The principles used are those of:

- observing practice;
- analysing the practice and applying theory which may have been derived from academic study, from research or from everyday experience;
- evaluating the curriculum;
- developing the curriculum;
- working as a team;
- involving the school's other teachers in the process.

In evaluating the nation wide application of IT-INSET practices, the evaluators conclude that tutors from training institutions tended to be the most influential members of the teams, an indication of the need to have someone who has time to reflect on research as well as on practice. The success of their work was also dependent on the extent to which the headteacher understood the principles of IT-INSET and made sure that the school collaborated in the process. This is clearly an exercise in partnership, and in reflective practice. The team avers that this project has considerably influenced DES thinking and the development of the CATE criteria.

The second research project, also DES funded, was entitled 'School-based training in the PGCE'. It was directed by Professor Paul Hirst and based at the University of Cambridge. This research project did not set out to evaluate or test out a particular form of teacher education, but rather to examine the context of teacher education, to study four Postgraduate Certificate of Education (PGCE) courses with a view to establishing the underlying principles of school-based training and to develop policy implications for future development. The project team recognized at the outset that there was both a professional and a political context to the idea of partnership in teacher education. The professional context was the advocacy by professional groups like the teacher unions, the Council for National Academic Awards (CNAA), the Universities Council for the Education of Teachers (UCET), of closer collaborations with schools in the task of teacher education. Hirst himself had come to the view that teachers as practitioners were able to develop what he called 'practical theories' of teaching which could come close to Schön's 'artistry'. The political context was the view adopted by government that the education system was failing the economy and the fault could be traced to the teacher educators who were not practical enough (Furlong et al, 1988), hence the demand for partnership to emphasize the role of school-based training.

The project team distinguished between four levels or forms of training:

- direct practice: direct experience of teaching in schools;
- indirect practice: training in practical matters (eg the use of computers) which takes place in the training institutions;
- the study of the principles of practice and their use which can take place in schools but also in the training institutions
- the critical study of practice and its principles in the light of fundamental theory and research. Again, this could take place in either school or college, but is more likely to take place in the latter.

The team argued that in the training process, practising teachers were best able to undertake the supervision of direct practice. Other aspects of training were probably best undertaken by the lecturers in the training institutions or in school according to circumstances, with the collaboration of teachers where possible. It was felt that teachers in schools would probably need in-service training to undertake the supervision of school practice and the examination of the principles of practice.

The third project forms the subject of a book by Tickle (1987) and is also concerned with partnership. This is an account of an experimental teacher-training course at the University of East Anglia which started in 1981 and is said to be inspired by Stenhouse's view of the teacher as a researcher (Stenhouse, 1975).

Research-based initial teacher education assumes that from the start of a professional career student teachers should, together with their tutors and practising teachers, be committed to the ideals of a unified research model (Tickle, 1987).

I am not too sure how students can commit themselves to such a model from the start, particularly as these were BEd students whose experience, when the course starts, must be limited. Passing over what may be rhetoric, the course shows certain similarities with others which involve the concept of the reflective practitioner and partnerships with schools. The book offers a number of case studies which are interesting in themselves, but the descriptive format adopted makes it difficult to distil any principles of practice of general applicability. There have been a number of other theoretical or empirical studies of teacher education schemes, for example, Kirk (1985), Lucas (1988), and Ashcroft and Griffiths (1989) all of which are concerned with partnership and reflective teaching, but in my view do nothing to modify the essence of this form of teacher education.

Rethinking teacher education

If Wragg could complain in 1982 that teacher education was not a field that had attracted many researchers, he could not do so today. There has been a minor explosion of studies in this country, not to mention the USA where Zeichner has perhaps taken the lead in developing work in this area. In examining all these proposals and research projects, I am conscious that many writers preface their studies with such words as 'teacher education is a problematic area', by which I understand that none see a simple or single answer to the question, how should we train or educate those embarking on a career in teaching?

Clearly, in the 1980s certain themes recurred: the insistence on the centrality of practice, the need for partnership with school, the development of practical theories or principles; so much so that I am inclined to wonder how many are climbing on a bandwagon that, given the political context, may yield dividends in research grants and approval of courses by CATE. Professor David Hargreaves has joined the chorus and regularly advocates school-based training in the pages of the *Times Educational Supplement*. What is surprising is that the idea of partnership, and to some extent the practice of partnership, has always been in existence in England and Wales. No teacher training could possibly have taken place without the schools cooperating and providing places for students. The quality of this partnership was variable from school to school, but schools were neither financed nor necessarily encouraged by their LEAs to participate more actively in the training process. They may be more willing to do so today, but they are certainly no more able to do so, given the tasks they have to undertake after the Education Reform Act of 1988.

Accepting, however, that teaching practice is central to teacher education, what is perhaps more worrying is the lack of a satisfying intellectual framework to underpin the practice of teacher education. To my mind the only really viable analysis made is that made by Schön in relation to professions as a whole. But this model needs to be elaborated in the context of the teaching profession, without making it too complicated, making sure that the practices advocated relate to the basic model.

Essentially we need to create a reflective practitioner. But a reflective practitioner needs something to reflect upon, hence the need to involve him or her in practice in a non-threatening way early on in the training. S/he needs to understand what reflection-in-action means. So someone – whether teacher-tutor or tutor – needs to be seen teaching and then analysing what went on and what quick decisions were taken and why. But this also shades off into reflection-after-action, which the student

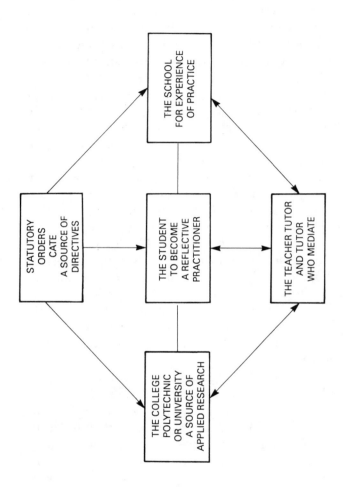

Figure 4.1 *An interactive system of teacher education*

can begin to practise after some experience of teaching. However, more repeated experience without some external input may not lead to improvement. Hence the need to feed in some of the findings of applied educational research, for example the findings about class management, mixed-ability teaching, questioning and explaining from the Teacher Education Project. These may help to modify teaching procedures in the next experience of practice.

To my mind teacher education needs to be an interactive system in which the student derives know-how of teaching from direct experience in school and from the findings of research which may well be derived from previous work in schools. But this learning needs to be mediated and organized by someone familiar with both the world of practice and that of research, which is where the teacher–tutor and tutor come in (see Figure 4.1). There are of course practical and financial problems to be solved before such a system can become a reality. As we saw with the IT–INSET scheme, six students, one tutor and one teacher is an expensive way of undertaking such teacher education. Given the pressures that teachers are under, given the shortage of teachers in certain subjects and certain geographical areas, it is difficult to see the schools being able, even if they are willing, to devote resources to such training schemes. The articled-teacher scheme will, when it operates, give us some empirical data to work on.

Chapter 5

Equality and Childhood: Education and the Myths of Teacher Training

Dennis O'Keeffe

Introduction: the intellectual crisis

Teacher education in Great Britain faces a period of upheaval. The ensuing uncertainty is perhaps in general no different from that obtaining in the education system as a whole. It arises partly from the deep sense of crisis which pervades education, and partly from the disruptive intrusions of a government dedicated to action but lacking a clear sense of what that action should be. This is true both of the preparation of teachers and the conduct of schools. The lack of vision, and therefore of real conviction, is apparent in the timidity displayed in some areas, compared to the brutal intrusion effected in others. One might cite the dithering over what should be done in English or mathematics and other crucial subjects, alongside the gratuitous destruction of the very successful O level (Sexton, 1988).

In addition to sharing in the general anxieties of education, however, teacher preparation labours under its own special disquiet. What has never really been settled is exactly what sort of activity teacher preparation is. Is it 'training' or 'education'? For decades· the matter has been unresolved. In the 1970s it was decided that the preparation of teachers should be entitled 'teacher education', presumably on the admirable grounds that education is more elevated than training. In recent years, with no official edict of change, the 'training' designation has reasserted itself. The change may be favoured by government but no formal decision has ever been taken. The reversion is in the event regrettable. One of the central errors of modern education is its 'technicist' ideology. There is no evidence that the art of teaching can be taught by one person to another. By contrast, experience shows that many clever people can *educate* other people.

The point is in essence a conceptual rather than an empirical one. The teacher is fundamentally an educator. An educator must be *educated*. The preparation of truck drivers or brain surgeons may constitute training. That of teachers has by definition to be educational. Getting students ready to teach children is essentially an educative activity, a view which needs to be reinstated. The opposite obtains, however. The technicist mythology seems set – along with other even worse solecisms – to prosper still further. True, primary teacher education now involves compulsory study of academic subjects. This is much to the credit of the Department of Education and Science (DES), working through the Committee for the Accreditation of Teacher Education (CATE). By definition CATE's insistence predicates an alarming hostility to traditional subjects in the preparing institutions; and in fact the overall trend is still the other way. The dropping of theory courses removes the one element of sustained intellectual inquiry that most primary B.Ed students had formerly to study.

Overall, however, the current rearranging of teacher education is actually slight, certainly compared to the vast restructuring of the work of schools as a result of the National Curriculum and the 1988 Education Reform Act. Two comments on the contrast seem pertinent. First, teacher education needs as much rearranging as does compulsory education. Secondly, what neither needs is the National Curriculum, an intemperate exercise in bureaucratic centralism, embarked on just when the case against large-scale institutional socialism seems incontrovertibly established. Such bureaucratization is a sad substitute for ameliorative action, and liable in the event to exacerbate the maladies it purports to cure. Nothing is being done, either in the schools or the preparing institutions, to halt the gradual deintellectualizing, over several decades, of our educational life. Sad to relate, the government seems not remotely to understand the crisis which faces us, nor its component parts and their inter relations.

Given the unprecedented public anxiety about education today, I should lay out my own worries unambiguously. The truth is that British education is gripped by a crisis of alarming proportions. It is an *intellectual* crisis, rooted in the partial subversion of our educational life by egalitarian, technicist and romantic ideologies. True, these ideologies do not live entirely comfortably together. Some of the exotic cultures we are enjoined to regard as 'equal', maintain an entirely unequal view of women, and a most unromantic view of childhood. Admittedly such contradiction is not unique to this new ideological mishmash. All civilization involves the coexistence of imperatives which are partly incompatible, as this chapter will maintain. But the ferocious and multiple contradictions of progressive educational ideology surpass all reason. This ideology is no more nor less than modern education's socialist disposition, and by definition out of tune with the real world. An immensely important part of our economic life and our civil order is regulated by a system which does not work properly.

The economic inefficiency is just par for the course. Like all publicly funded activity, state education has probably always been inefficient. Till recently, however, its socialism has been mainly institutional, a mixture of public finance, quasi-monopoly and compulsory attendance. These conditions constitute a suppliers' dream. Since the 1960s, however, they have been supplemented by socialism of the ideological–angst sort, the only socialist intellection available now that the Marxist paradigm has collapsed.

For years we have been transmitting wrong notions of acceptable education. We have been wrong about English, wrong about mathematics, wrong about science, wrong about history, wrong about languages, wrong about culture. I cannot argue the case at length here. But look-say reading is a disaster (McNee, 1989). Spelling, syntax and traditional literary values do matter and are being neglected. Mathematics is an analytical and not an empirical subject. History is not advanced by feeble empathizing with the lower orders of the past; nor can untutored minds engage in historical 'research'. In sum, the traditional subjects are today either neglected or assaulted at their very core (O'Keeffe, 1986).

Most crucial of all, we have been wrong about morality and citizenship, and about educational achievement and its pains and rewards (Lynn, 1988). We have been mistaken about our whole intellectual tradition and the prerequisites of our future prospects. And, crucially, teacher education is the single most important redoubt of these manifold errors.

The education mutation

There has occurred a curious mutation in 'educated' thought in the Western societies in recent decades. The numbers of communists and fellow-travellers have shrunk drastically. But objectively the enemies of our civilization have been more than compensated for by an increasing inclination on some people's part to interfere with other citizens' lives, combined with a growing moral and political cynicism. The new ideology is amorphous and shambling, but nonetheless threatening. It combines a collapse of faith in our own traditions and way of life, with the adoption of a set of sentimental and strident campaigns about race, gender and culture. These campaigns are seen as achievable through the employment of a technicist approach to socialization, which conceives it effectively as a moralistic technology. The egalitarians seem to hold that the 'equal opportunities' person can be produced to order by a set of specifiable measures, such as those aimed at the abolition of competitive striving and stress. For example, streaming can be abolished, as can nerve-racking unseen examinations. Direct instillation of the adopted values, on the other hand, can be affected by the endless and unchallenged drumming into children of the appropriate slogans. The conformity of the teachers concerned can be assured through 'self-awareness' programmes or even spying, à la Brent.

The welcome eclipse of silly views of China and so on, has been accompanied by a dangerous erosion of belief in our own institutions, except for certain new ones set up to enforce the new orthodoxies. The whole benighted disposition is compounded by a perverse ignorance of history and of the nature and urgency of wealth-creation (Dawson, 1981). Not since the seventeenth century have people in this country seemed inclined to such baroque credulity in such numbers.

The contemporary radical disposition will surely be looked back on with astonishment. It combines intolerable bossiness with intellectual collapse. It celebrates the person and his or her rights but deprecates individual responsibilities, in effect delegating them to the state. It is deeply antinomian and self-doubting. It dismisses, or invades and distorts, religion. Yet alongside this unprecedented rejection of our tradition we find a strange set of ugly certainties.

In its extremer forms, which in the case of some British LEAs, for example, are sadly commonplace, our contemporary educational radicalism castigates males, whites and policemen as well as big business. It repudiates traditional patriotism and yet it rejoices in transferred nationalisms. Though faith in international communism has waned drastically, there are continuing attempts in 'development education' to legitimate new tyrannies. The kind of intellectual who once put his loyalty at the disposal of the Soviets or Communist China, now sides with the ANC or the nationalist-Marxist guerrillas of Latin America. Such attitudes are the very stuff of the courses promoted by educationalists like Robin Richardson and David Selby (Scruton, 1985). Interest is typically to be displaced from its rooted position in what is one's own, and relocated, a point that remains true even of that majority of educational progressives who have no faith in Nicaragua and such experiments. Our radicalism rejects long-established cultural enthusiasms and at the same time it pursues an intellectually feeble multiculturalism, whose only real energy has been in the creation of 'jobs for the persons' and the identification of enemies.

Just what causes this self-doubt and this transfer of conviction to wayward or sinister causes, we do not know; probably it relates to the decline in religious belief. Its genesis is mysterious, though it has some roots in Rousseau, and has to be seen as a modern version of our age-old misanthropy. Unlike the coherent revolutionism of the first half of our century, this new disgruntlement is only tenuously attached to Marxism. Many of its exponents would, indeed, disown any such label. In this sense world studies and development studies, with their residual neo-Marxism, are not typical of the socialist intelligentsia of education. Certainly the glad confident morning of revolution seems quite banished. The missionizing is now mostly a series of sour notes in the public sector. There is now not even the pretence of a real economic theory. Education is the real world of those activists who know at least that world revolution is a faded dream. Education will just have to do, now that the real thing has failed to come along.

In any event we find here a bizarre pattern of malice and naïveté. It is as ostensibly unlikely an accompaniment to modern rationalism as the witchcraft craze was to the Renaissance. If ever one wanted a demonstration of Hayek's 'fatal conceit' then surely this is it (Hayek, 1988). The huge 'planned' Robbins-sanctioned expansion of higher education has come to this: thousands and thousands of men and women have passed through the system and, instead of the humane scepticism that an enlightened society should expect, we find a wide-ranging credulity. Teacher education is the most important relay for getting this perverse outlook from higher education to the schools.

The government view

The irony is that the government knows quite well that a lot is wrong. It just has not managed to grasp it deeply or comprehensively enough. Partly this is a matter of asking the wrong people. You cannot handle the analysis of civilization itself if you consult its enemies overmuch, especially if they have done their homework better than you. The government has been asking the very worst people, the civil servants. What the government seems to understand by our educational troubles is very simply put. We have here a practical crisis. There has been too much educational theory, too much Marxism. Old-fashioned British pragmatism will soon put this right. Cut out the theory (done); make initial teacher 'training' more 'practical' (done); and bring into this training people with more recent 'practical' experience (being done).

The situation is a very odd one. The government's reforming energies seem largely intact, and the leadership knows that action is needed in education. Most of the changes underway at present, however, indicate that the crisis is indeed seen as a *practical* one. The government is acting on the advice of Her Majesty's Inspectorate (HMI) and of the DES civil servants. Hence all we need, apparently, is a good dose of old-fashioned British empiricism. This explains the strengthening of the CATE machinery and the decision to rely heavily on experienced front-line teachers in the reformation of teacher education.

We seem to be reduced to old-fashioned muddling through. Admittedly it is very difficult for any government relying on bad advice to understand our complex educational reality. There is such a confusing maze of truth and error to be negotiated. It is especially hard to get through the tangle of half-truths, lies and evasions created by the educational syndicalists of the DES and the inspectorates. Can you confidently ask the barber if you need a haircut, or the mugger which are the safe streets? As for teacher educators, they are such devoted 'progressives' that their prescriptions are inevitably one-sided. They are committed to 'equal opportunities' almost to a person. So things scarcely look promising.

The broad context of teacher education

Teacher education belongs to a set of vital activities which cannot be analysed satisfactorily outside their much wider contexts. This is not a cliche; if it were, teacher education would be recognized as just such an issue. It is in the event not recognized, unfortunately, that to question one vital element (eg teacher education), in the complex web of educational arrangements is often to raise controversy over many other elements too. Almost nowhere in the literature is there to be found any treatment of the preparation of teachers which stresses its systemic context.

In fact, teacher education, or 'teacher training' as it is now called, by a reversal to earlier technicist aspiration quite characteristic of our age, cannot be satisfactorily analysed even in the most preliminary sense, outside a comprehensive consideration of our intellectual and cultural arrangements. Any developed treatment of the issues has clearly to delve into the different institutions involved – primary schools, secondary schools, and the various colleges within and outside universities and polytechnics, where teachers are prepared – and see how these are connected with each other and with LEAs and the inspectorates. All this is complex enough. But really to come to grips with a complex reality, any sophisticated account must also deal with questions of epistemology and of socio-economy. It seems hard to imagine that reasonable policies could be forthcoming without this comprehensive approach. Sad to say, it also seems unlikely that such wide-ranging theoretical questions have ever featured prominently in British educational decision-making.

This is not an advocacy of large-scale planning, merely the observation of interrelatedness. What is happening and why? We have a crisis in our education system which threatens our very civilization. We need to understand this. Hayek's fulminations against 'constructivist rationalism' (Hayek, 1988) do not preclude an in-depth examination of complex social phenomena. Education has had the opposite problem – very ambitious schemes, like the whole network of egalitarian planning, without much serious study, as opposed to copious ideologizing. Such planning has given us comprehensive schools and the GCSE. These are reversals to more primitive forms, to lesser degrees of intellectual differentiation. No civilization really serious about making its way in the world would have contemplated such atavistic moves; but there are undoubtedly more such 'advances' in the egalitarian pipeline. For example, the A level is under threat (Debenham, 1989).

The ambiguities of education

Education is inherently complicated enough, without the contradictions which socialism visits on anything it touches. Education has fundamentally two instructional functions, which live precariously side by side. There is first of all integration, or making us a community, stressing our common citizenship and heritage. This is a very difficult function, given the sizeable minority of children who are inadequately or deviantly socialized at home (Segalman and Marsland, 1989) and, at least in some areas, the multicultural pattern of citizenship today. In contradistinction to this imperative of integration, there is a differentiating function. A complex division of labour cannot function without its participants having access to knowledge of the distribution of talent. The imperative here is to sort us out. Education takes to itself the business of finding out, and developing, our differentially distributed abilities. It must then publicize them through such mechanisms as certification. This is a function which cannot be abrogated in any economy whose citizens wish to prosper (Dore, 1976). The poor societies of the past had undifferentiated populations whose talents had not been discovered and furthered. This defined in good measure their poverty.

The difficulty of this historically novel imperative of talent-spotting is that it hurts. It entails winners and losers. The trouble with competitions, as Orwell once said, is that somebody wins them (Orwell, 1970). The trouble with progressive education, we might respond today, is that it acts as if an unkind world will go away if we let the children play forever.

Teacher education is therefore party to the difficulties from both ends. In its current insistence that we are perennially divided between the two sexes, and today between the many races and cultures which now inhabit this country, as if these ascriptions and attributions were more important than our common citizenship, teacher education tends to threaten the integrative function. By its hostility to intellectual hierarchy, it compromises education's differentiating function. Teacher education thus sits at the heart of our intellectual crisis. It transmits throughout primary and secondary education a series of perverse signals, enjoining on us separation where we need togetherness, and homogeneity where differentiation is required. Unless all this is checked and reversed, it spells danger to us all in two obvious ways. There may be those who have been taught to despise the civil order as 'racist', 'sexist' and 'ethnocentric'. Some of them may not make the best of citizens. It does not take many alienated young men to cause a wholly disproportionate amount of trouble. Alternatively there may be rebellion against the civil order by those who have nothing valuable to bring to market after 11 compulsory years of school. Indeed, there may well be individuals who are alienated as a result of both of these experiences. It is likely that some of the unacceptable behaviour of young British males does indeed derive from both these perversities. In combination these two risks could add up to national decline.

The standards controversy

This question of crisis by no means reduces to that of the standards achieved by children in school. Indeed, once one has established that our school standards are too low, one has done no more than enter the real discussion. It is worth repeating, however, that our standards are lamentable (Cox, Marks, Pomian-Srzednicki, 1983). Indeed, they are the empirics of our intellectual crisis. Even allowing for the difficulties of international comparison, the case that our education lags dramatically behind that of the Japanese, for example, is quite overwhelming (Lynn, 1988). The real oddity is that so many people seem willing to deny this shortfall. It is true that proof of historically falling domestic standards is not available, though as Colin Coldman points out, if steps are taken to force standards down, down they will go (Coldman, 1989; Debenham, 1989). What seems incontestable is that the present standards achieved by our schools are quite inadequate for today's world (Lynn, 1988). This is a fact which needs more public recognition if the larger issue of intellectual crisis is to be addressed.

The standards picture is a very mixed one. There are two main truths, the domestic and the international. The domestic truth is the less harsh; after all, on our home patch education functions brilliantly for a minority of people, well for a lot more and adequately for many millions. It is the huge minority for whom it functions very badly who have to be our main reforming concern. The defensive, syndicalist interest is bound to point to the brilliant–good–adequate end of the performance spectrum, as typifying the whole. This is one good reason for refusing to contain the discussion in purely domestic terms.

The international truth summons up a harsher indictment. True, the evidence for our inferior performance vis-à-vis other Western systems is by no means overwhelming. In mathematics and science we seem to be about halfway up the performance hierarchy. Significantly we seem to be well behind the Germans (Prais and Wagner, 1985). This effort is not good enough, clearly, but its inadequacy sinks into our consciousness properly only when we recognize the starkly unacceptable character of the Western academic performance as a whole. We have to compare ourselves to the Japanese. Theirs is the qualitatively different performance. Japan is an economic superpower, if not at present then probably soon. When all the reservations have been made, there seems little reason to deny Professor Lynn's judgement that the Japanese teach their children much more successfully than we do ours. In the case of mathematics the evidence is overwhelming. But the Japanese also take a much more robust and less agonized approach to moral training than we do. Certainly, as Lynn points out, both private and public morality are stressed in Japanese schools (Lynn, 1988).

The crisis is intellectual, not practical

Standards, however damning an index of performance, are only surface evidence. The real crisis lies beneath. The conviction has taken hold, especially among teacher educators, that education should be a prime vehicle for the transmission of a comprehensive egalitarianism. There has been much cant about 'equality of opportunity' at school, although this is a chimera unless its proponents can prevent parents helping their children in various ways. This would be hard to enforce in a free society, though socialist despotisms have been good at flattening some hierarchies (Wiles, 1977). In practice, the equal-opportunity obsession has meant that inequalities in performance are regarded as intolerable, and are themselves seen as indicative of unequal opportunities (O'Keeffe, 1985).

Equality is the motor of most of today's hate-cults. It reverberates, for example, in an incoherent multiculturalism, informing such saws as 'All cultures are equal'. It is hard for anyone educated to believe this could actually be said. But such nonsense, which offers deep comfort to ignorance, is widely taught (Swift, 1972). There has also been an attempt to equalize children and adults. A cult of childhood has been agitated into place, one as bad in its way as our ancestors' view that childhood was an inconvenience to be got through as soon as possible. Today in many educational circles, and especially in teacher education, childhood is held to be a near-sacred condition, with priority over the claims of intellectual tradition. Childhood must be free from stressful competition; nor must children learn alienating ideas about hierarchies and differentially distributed abilities (Bernstein, 1977). Nothing must hurt, nothing must tax, nothing must reveal intractable dullness. In practice this can only mean that brilliance is not welcome. One has only to look at BEd, and PGCE programmes up and down the country to see what a grip this kind of thinking has. It is apparent that teacher education has been a main conduit for getting this ideological fare into our schools. The question is scarcely debatable; presumably the defenders of this ideology would not deny but proclaim their efforts, seeing as virtue what to me is vice.

More innocent in intention, but just as bad in its effects, is the ideology of technique and practice – sometimes known as 'technicism' – which holds that teachers can be 'trained' like so many technicians, just as pupils can readily be equipped with 'skills'. Teacher educators have always and understandably succumbed to a little technical hubris. Today, when so-called techniques and skills are confused with education itself, the technicist illusion multiplies. Such an error disastrously demotes the intellectual functions of education. Indeed we now have a 'skills' mania on our hands (Palmer, 1986). In sum we have institutionalized wrong ideas about what children are and need, and about what things teachers should teach and how, alongside wrong ideas as to how teachers should be got ready for teaching. These ills are the origin of our standards woes.

The crisis is unprecedented. Not since the introduction of compulsory education in 1870 has there been such a dire condition in our educational arrangements. Government has unfortunately failed to recognize this. Nowhere is this blindness more apparent than in teacher education, where it is not even admitted that there is a crisis, save of physical bodies and resources. The emphasis on more assessment, more teachers with recent experience, more practical know-how, causes no offence in this corner of academe. But if the crisis is intellectual, the move to practical emphasis will effect nothing worthwhile. It will merely result in the more efficient transmission of error. It will make things worse. It is better that error be inefficiently transmitted.

Intellectual errors cannot be corrected practically. Some LEAs have been subverted. Some practice is wildly wrong. What is to be gained from colluding with such practitioners in an unreformed posture? And even if the intellectual errors were recognized, we could not in practice improve matters very quickly using the assumptions which govern teacher education at present. We would also have to shed the idea that 'experts' can teach other people how to teach. There is no evidence that the core of teaching as a craft can be transmitted from one person to another; it is much better to concentrate on the transmission of knowledge than on fantasies about training. Successful teaching depends on abilities which elude specification. These abilities are actually mysterious and diffuse, indeed much more so than those of carpentry or surgery, for example.

Education is inherently contradictory

Even in the most elevated education system conceivable, the pursuit of truth, rationality and moral goodness, to some extent will vie, as principles, with the claims of national cultural tradition and with the banausic demands of the division of labour. This may be expected to produce contradiction and discord to some degree. Education is in this regard to be seen in something of the same light as art, with its tolerance of ambiguity.

Now, however, a special and historically novel kind of incoherence has been visited upon the world of school. Increasingly larger and more voracious claims of equality and childhood are installed. Their earlier victories, such as destreaming the primary schools and getting rid of the grammar schools, have been joined by the more strident sub-Marxisms of the present. The New Jerusalem ethos, which Correlli Barnett shows the elite trying to impose on us educationally since the nineteenth century (Barnett, 1986), has proved protean, whatever its intellectual shortcomings. The fatal decade of the 1960s, in which so many voices were raised against our heritage, when so many nihilisms were pitted against our traditional morality, equipped our educational zealots with powerful emotional ammunition. The movement successfully tapped into the reservoir of guilt which Orwell long ago discerned in the educated British (Orwell, 1970). There is now a vast apparatus, apparent inside and outside the education system, which promotes the insatiable moralisms of race, gender, multiculture and childhood. Teacher education is notable here, claiming to possess a set of techniques which can produce teachers, with the confidence engineers feel about machines.

Admittedly the claims of rationality, high culture, national tradition and jobs, whatever their internal relations, have in any case never been given free reign. One part of our tragic educational history is that we have never demanded enough of our young citizens at school. There has never been a real attempt either to make the curriculum a vehicle for the dissemination of high culture, or to organize the pre-work learning of young people on German lines. Professor Musgrove, for example, maintains that there has long been a determined effort to minimize the influence of the division of labour (Musgrove, 1978). The difference since the 1960s is that there are now powerful voices raised in positive favour of ignorance. Another unwelcome development is the widespread disposition to denigrate all things British.

Whatever grip the traditional educational principles might have achieved, in rivalry or harmony, has now been loosened further by the advent of these ideological newcomers, the hydra-headed cults of egalitarianism, self-hatred and infancy. There is no empirical problem here. It is not, as some conservatives believe, Marxism which is the trouble with teacher education. Readers can easily confirm this by asking for course details at any institution of teacher preparation. I will not single out any institution; but equality-mongering and the hate-cults, in conjunction with the celebration of childhood hegemony are the threat today, not Marxism.

Those who believe that schooling is about subjects and about learning facts, theories, values and techniques, as the necessary but not sufficient conditions of education, are fighting back. In the case of teacher education, unfortunately, they are mostly fighting back from outside the activity (O'Hear, 1988; Hillgate, 1989). The fight continues and none of us knows how it will end. It is this warring of principles, a conflict in which, at least temporarily, victory seems to have gone to the side of equality and childhood, which has generated our present educational crisis. The crisis in teacher education is simply a special and very intense version of our general educational crisis. This general crisis not merely embraces the preparation of teachers; it even centres on it. The most urgent attention needs to be given to its repair.

The problem of interests

Ideological fantasies have been able to gain such a strong and disfiguring hold because of the peculiar socio-economy of our educational system, which empowers a clique of unrepresentative intellectuals and disenfranchises most other citizens. This minority grip on the means of cultural transmission is revealed in the relative paucity of the debate on teacher education. The curricular elite, having gravely compromised our education system, in the process threatening both our economic life and our civil order, continue to control teacher education almost without let or hindrance. The much smaller group of writers hostile to our present educational dispensation has not been able to set out the wider debate needed. What is really indicated is radical assessment of our politically adverse arrangements for the preparation of teachers.

The teachers are not to blame

The late Herbert Marcuse called education in capitalist societies 'moronizing'. It is odd when Marxists and conservatives agree. If we are looking for the authors of our feeble British version, however, we should not dwell long with the teachers. They are the principal transmitters of an unsatisfactory education, but – far from being its beneficiaries – they are among its principal victims. The teachers are a demoralised labour force, badly remunerated and accorded low status. Out of a limited budget the 'plums' have been snatched by a syndicalist group involving only very senior teachers, the local and national inspectorates, teacher educators and educational civil servants, again local and national, and the union bosses.

This syndicalist group has immense power and almost unlimited access to media publicity. It is the embodiment of Karl Mannheim's dream that an intelligentsia, blended judiciously from Plato and Marx, should regulate other people's lives (Mannheim, 1954). In the event this curricular elite has mostly preferred, as its mentors, Rousseau and Dewey; but its influence has probably exceeded Mannheim's most extravagant hopes. The endless propaganda it puts out in defence of its interest is the main obstacle between the British nation and the educational renaissance we need if we are not to witness our economic resurgence aborted for lack of real skills and qualifications. Nor is the reestablishment of our Western intellectual tradition the most vital task, crucial though it is. Even more important is the role education will have to play in the coming decades if we are to restore to our civil order that authority which once made our country the envy of others.

Today's crisis: education, civil order and the market

The issue of civil order is of paramount importance. It is characteristic of modern societies that they entrust part of the burden of creating the mental climate necessary to support civil order to the historically new mechanism of mass education. If this mass education should prove in any deep sense inadequate, disaster can threaten. It is a commonplace that modern political totalitarian systems have always identified education as a prime target for subversion. To debauch a community's intellectual life is the surest way to undermine it (McNamara and O'Keeffe, 1988).

From the beginning mass education has been less than satisfactory in the free societies. First of all, it is publicly financed, which is another way of saying inefficiently organised. Next, much of it is compulsory – in Great Britain the minimum leaving age has gone up twice since the Second World War, to its present level of 16 years; and during the heavy unemployment of the first half of the 1980s the various youth-training programmes effectively hiked it up again. There may be a case for compulsion, though it would have to be across a much more modest stretch than the manic eleven years now demanded of all boys and girls in this country, whatever their abilities and inclinations. The trouble with compulsion is that it lays a very heavy bureaucratic hand on what most people would do anyway, and inevitably switches power away from compelled citizens and towards those doing the compelling: the educational elite. To reduce the citizens' discretion in this way is to threaten the consent in which their political obligation is grounded.

This educational compulsion is a vital link in the process whereby power passes to suppliers. The citizens are taxed and the proceeds handed over to 'experts'; to compound the offence their children have to attend the institutions which the experts provide. None of these deficiencies is in itself definitive of failure. However, public finance and compulsion obtain in Japanese education, which, if not economically efficient, is at least very effective – though it ought to be noted that Japan has an unusually large number of private and very successful secondary schools (Lynn, 1988). Circumstances in this country are different from those of Japan. The crisis which now threatens British education involves a specific new aspect – new since the 1960s that is. This is the fracture in general outlook between the educational decision-makers and the public at large. Broadly speaking the key educational decision-makers are now socialist: paradoxically, just when the public at large has rejected socialism. The personnel in teacher education tend to favour all the main socialist doctrines. The DES is itself a notoriously socialist ministry. The inspectors, local and HMI, have also tended to advance egalitarian and 'progressive' educational causes. The same is true of the Society of Education Officers (Sexton, 1988). This massive contradiction, between a non-socialist public and a largely socialist class of educationalists and education administrators, defines our educational predicament.

There is undoubtedly a tendency to radical intellectual pluralism in all the advanced societies. In itself it is desirable and anyway inevitable. Markets can probably contain it. But what if extreme, socialist or even antinomian opinion bunches up in the public sector? The fact is that this is precisely what seems to have happened in British education, and in the United States, and in many other countries. In time Japan too may expect to feel the deleterious effects of child-centred revolution and the campaign for all-purpose equality – unless she profits from our mistakes, that is.

The two educational socialisms

The Orwellian suspicion of socialist intellectuals has been justified in the educational case. The trick, therefore, is to keep their influence out of school classrooms. This is not easy in a free society like ours. For one thing our educational dilemma is not mainly a matter of general ill-will. There is plenty of that about, too; plenty of intellectuals would love to fracture the value consensus without which a capitalist economy and a democratic society cannot function. Mostly, however, the evil is not deliberate, but a gradual yielding to managerial temptations, such as social engineering and spiritual manipulation. However good their intentions, suppliers will be almost irresistibly tempted to set their own agenda. This is probably acceptable as long as the public and the teachers/suppliers agree on what that agenda/curriculum should be. If they do not agree, there are grounds for trouble and discord. In free societies, there are only weak mechanisms of enforcement in predominantly publicly financed areas such as education in the event of supplier waywardness. The public sector has a poor track record in terms of consumer sovereignty.

The adoption of antinomian, egalitarian and romantic attitudes has converted the merely institutional socialism of our educational arrangements into something more positively socialist. This has happened since the never-to-be-sufficiently-regretted 1960s. Before then, though it was economically bound to be inefficient – lacking, as all public monopolies do, any proper mechanism of rewards for efficiency and penalties for failure – education tended to tick over, to get by, to suffice. There was even, from 1945 until the 1960s, a limited surrogate for market differentiation, in the form of the 11-plus. This was arbitrary regionally, and by no means always accurate; but it was a mid-school marker of performance. Now there is none. And in any case the transition is a bigger one than the removal of one crude performance indicator would effect. The people who ran pre-comprehensive education agreed, if on different intellectual levels, with the less-educated citizens whose children actually attended the institution. The state-financed education system, whatever its faults, coincided in its core values, those which pertain to the civil order, with the outlooks of most citizens. In this at least there was at school, if not consumer sovereignty, at any rate the political sovereignty of citizens.

Things are different now. Ideological infiltration since the 1960s has shifted the whole education system over towards socialism proper. We now have a system many of whose senior decision-makers prefer childhood to knowledge and equality to achievement. People with such convictions cannot educate other people to be teachers; they do not know what education is. Perhaps they can train people in false ideologies of childhood and so on. I doubt it, and I hope not. Such an aspiration is Pavlovian and ignoble. The battle continues and no one has won a total victory. It is impossible in any society where the division of labour is as important as it is in ours, for the hopes of citizens to be totally frustrated. The imperatives of the wider world, the demands of the job structure, the claims of genuine intellectual assessment, all do come through. But they are unacceptably compromised. They are filtered through, and partly muted by, the ideological socialism of which I write. The resulting synthesis or ensemble is partly dysfunctional in relation to the demands of a competitive free-enterprise economy. It is also inimical to the imperatives of a mature civil order.

What we now face, admittedly in comparative terms in a rather early phase, is a socialist crisis, belonging to the same generic order of inadequacy as the Soviet harvest. A wrong view of educationally significant knowledge and achievement has been established, paralleling the wrong understanding of the nature of economic activity characteristic of socialism. We simply cannot approach the future in such a manifestly deficient vessel. We must not encumber our posterity with so hopelessly inadequate an education system. The future international economy will be 'knowledge-intensive'. Those societies will best succeed which preserve the greatest intellectual triumphs of human history, which achieve thereby a proper justication of social order and a powerful accumulation of human capital. Any education system which devotes much time and energy to 'equality' or the romance of childhood, will just get left behind.

As the government seeks to revitalize education in general and teacher education in particular, these two aims – economic resurgence and the re-establishment of a civilized social control – must surely be the educational focus of Mrs Thatcher and her eventual successors.

The role of teacher education

The 'progressive' revolution has not fallen in on us from the sky, like false mannah. Teacher education piped it into the schools. Given the inherently inefficient economic structure of schools, the outcome has been to compound crisis. The near monopoly enjoyed by the state system effectively preempts the influence of the market, and suppresses in particular those monitoring processes which in private markets tend to distinguish good from bad, to reward success and to penalize failure.

One is talking about systemic failure on the whole, rather than personal culpability. But let us mingle the normative and positive paradigms here. Teachers are not primarily to blame for the crisis; they are more the victims than the authors of our educational malady. It is the syndicalist nexus of teacher educators, inspectors, union bosses and civil servants who have stitched them up. Promotion is witheld from non-conformists, and anyway pedagogic Solzhenitsyns are few; Olympians are a special breed, after all. Teacher educators are more culpable than teachers proper, as the relatively free must always be held more accountable than the brutally constrained. But it is the inspectorate and the civil servants who have played the most egregious part in this calamity. They are the freest, the least confined, the guiltiest link in the chain of decision-making. It is they who have visited upon our country's schools this intellectual farce, this amalgam of ignorance, guilt, envy and managerial hubris known as progressive education.

Clearly we need to spell out in detail the various components of teacher education. Until recently these could have been listed as follows:

1. Teaching practice.
2. Academic subject-matter.
3. Theoretical courses in education. The most important three here have been philosophy, psychology and sociology.
4. Methods courses.

The educational *bien-pensant* elite has now, however, introduced a replacing vocabulary or programme for teacher education. It bears no neat correspondence to the traditional package listed above, though the biggest change is easily grasped: the traditional 'theory' courses have been dropped. The other major innovation of recent years is the requirement that people doing primary BEd courses should be obliged to study some hard academic material, across an 18-month stretch. This isolated improvement reflects to the credit of the DES and CATE.

A May 1989 consultation document (DES, 1989c) gives us:

1. Students' school experience and teaching practice.
2. Curriculum studies in primary courses
3. Subject-studies and subject application to pupils' learning.
4. Education and professional studies.

It would be very interesting to try to investigate the impact for good and ill of these components, past and present. The fact is that many of the people who enter college are good, so it is hardly surprising if they are still good when they leave. There are others who improve enormously during the course. By definition these improvers on a grand scale should not be many – unless we are allowing a lot of weak people into initial training. In any case there is a real problem of identification involved.

If students improve during the course, which parts of it are they most benefiting from? If the teaching practice is crucial, then those critics who support the proposed apprenticeship approach would seem to have a good point. Students could learn as well or better in the classroom under the guidance of good teachers without going to college at all.

If the exposure to fierce academic standards is what matters, then it has to be said that this too could be done elsewhere. Those who say that a degree at a university or polytechnic is the thing, and not the 'training', would seem to be vindicated.

Does the theory make a difference? Obviously it cannot if there is none. There are strong grounds for arguing that education theory does not have a technical impact. The grounds for studying it are educational, and not based on any training considerations. Education theory is an important area of human concern, insofar as education itself is important. That is the ground for would-be teachers studying it. No one is making large claims for its intellectual accomplishments. Education theory is a low-status body of intellectual activity. Its predictive powers are weak. The fact is, however, that weak and frail though it be, it is all we have.

Civilization should have prosecuted its case more vigorously. There has been bad theory. The answer to bad theory might be no theory; but good theory would be better. I still hold that the philosophy, sociology, psychology and history of education, whatever their limitations, are crucial bodies of investigation, ignorance of which will make a teacher the poorer. If we are to retain formal initial teacher education it is absurd to excise theory from the programme. It has now been swept away, however, by a combination of conservative hostility, the self-indulgent behaviour of some of its exponents, especially in sociology, and most important of all, by the indifference of its worst former exponents who have now found different bows for their antinomian arrows.

It suits the book of the equal-opportunities mongers and ignorance salesmen to abandon theory now. The neo-Marxist case is in ruins; almost no one takes that seriously any more. Above all there is now a considerable anti-socialist literature to contend with. On theory courses the questions of race and so forth stood some chance of being treated as problematic. It is much better for those who have made up their minds in advance as to what they want children and students to believe, that these issues be removed from nominally academic courses. There they run the risk of a genuine confrontation with the pens of Flew or Scruton or Partington, incomparably better minds than those which curricular socialism has at its disposal (O'Keeffe, 1986). Far better to leave the sinking ship of theory and climb aboard the new-methods vessel so thoughtfully provided by Conservative magnanimity (or perhaps incompetence). There the hitherto precarious distemper now enjoys legal endorsement and the power which comes from depoliticization. Now the agitation literature can work as uncontested back-up for enshrined doctrine.

As to what are variously called professional or subject-application courses – what used to be called 'methods' courses – by which HMI and the rest of the educational establishment now set such great store, they are a highly suspect activity in more senses than one. Very few men and women seem to be able to make them work. They are the least popular of all courses in British teacher education. They are unproven and they are both easy to trivialize and easy to subvert. Almost nowhere is there any honest discussion of the general insubstantiality and frequent unpopularity of these courses. Nor have many voices identified the inherent weakness of such activities – namely that they are predicated on a false claim, the myth of transposable technique. Anyone who has worked in teacher education knows that the most common complaint is that 'they don't teach you how to teach.' Of course they do not; for the simple reason that they cannot. It cannot be done. One individual cannot teach another how to teach. An individual can teach another English or mathematics or science. Education theory can be taught and taught well. But teaching cannot. Unfortunately teacher educators have a vested interest in running away from this obvious truth. And so the cycle of frustration and disappointment continues across the decades.

This technicist myth coincides with a strange pattern of negligence. To say that one person cannot teach another how to teach is not to say that there are no practical things which could be done to good effect on a training course. We could teach voice-use for example. Maybe there are courses of education where students are taught to project and protect their voices; but this is certainly not standard practice. There is a tendency to neglect what could be done in favour of what cannot be done; or even in favour of what should not be done, for example multiculturalism.

As well as claiming to do what cannot be done, namely the teaching of the art of teaching, the methods specialist will often be a devotee of empirical mathematics, multiculturalism and the other malfunctions and dysfunctions of today. Add to this a common disposition to regard standards (spelling, etc) as irrelevant or elitist and you have a three-part mixture of 'expertise' to be sceptical about, comprising the technicist, the antinomian and the philistine. The epithet 'Marxist' is largely redundant. Anyway, are the Marxian myths notably worse than those of teacher education? In any event the nation's educational resurgence cannot even begin until we have removed from teacher education the debilitating myths of the present.

Chapter 6

The Necessity of Teacher Education

Keith Swanwick

Introduction

During the academic year 1988–9, attention focused quite sharply on initial teacher education. Proposals for 'licensed' and 'articled' teachers emanated from the Department of Education and Science (DES) with implications in particular for the Postgraduate Certificate in Education (PGCE) course. There was much criticism of the PGCE in the press and considerable correspondence about the value of such courses and the possibilities of basing training more centrally in schools, involving teachers as mentors and regarding students as apprentices. Partly in response to this, we carried out a small piece of research into the attitudes of our own students and of teacher colleagues in schools associated with the Institute of Education.

Misinterpreting evidence on teaching standards

A criticism of PGCE courses advanced in particular by Baroness Cox (1989) and Professor O'Hear (1988), is that Her Majesty's Inspectorate (HMI) reports on teacher ineffectiveness are evidence of poor initial training. Our attention is drawn to the *The New Teacher in School* (Department of Education Science, 1988c), the HMI report in which we are told that 25 per cent of lessons taken by newly qualified teachers are less than satisfactory. In other words, 75 per cent are presumed to be satisfactory. Considering the inevitable strains of the probationary year and the failure to implement the James Report by supporting probationary teachers to the extent of giving them half a timetable this seems hardly surprising, if regrettable. The report on secondary schools, 1988 – *Secondary Schools* (Department of Educational Science, 1988b) – shows that probationary teachers taught for 81.5 per cent of the week against the average 83.3 for scale 1 and 2 teachers.) But we have to notice that the estimate of 25 per cent 'unsatisfactory' lessons is not confined to teachers in their first year. Concern has been expressed by HMI about the quality of work of some teachers with many years of classroom experience. Take, for instance *Standards in Education, 1987–88*, the annual report of HMI Chief Inspector of Schools (Department of Educational Science, 1989a). Here, in the context of a favourable reference to the GCSE we are told: 'Four lessons out of five were judged to be satisfactory or better in our recent report (GCSE), a higher proportion than is usually reported in our inspection findings.' In other words, 20 per cent of the teaching was thought unsatisfactory and this was considered an improvement on the usual performance of teachers where around 25 per cent of observed teaching tends to be below an acceptable level. What are we to make of this? Is it reasonable to expect probationary teachers to perform *better* than teachers in general, most of whom would have had substantial experience? Is experience by itself likely to bring about better standards?

The only inference we can draw from this much-cited 'evidence' is that classroom experience *by itself* appears to be no guarantee of effective professional practice. Yet experience is recommended by Cox and others as the only useful element of training courses. The rest of the PGCE course is seen as so much 'theory' with a bias towards certain sociological 'fads'. The dangerous half truth is perpetuated that 'the only way to learn how to teach is by doing it.'

If we really probe the data assembled by HMI we might also notice that less than ten qualified teachers each year fail to pass their probationary period; a minute proportion. Working at the levels of interpretation that characterize the arguments of Cox and others, this could be seen to imply either that the HMI has standards that are too high or that those responsible for the probationary year – heads, most particularly heads of department and to some extent LEA officers – have low expectations or poor judgement. If we assume the former then the proportion of new teachers giving 'satisfactory' lessons may be even higher than 75 per cent; if the latter, then this would severely erode any confidence in entrusting the whole of the training and assessment of student teachers to schools. How can such a massive proportion of new teachers be considered to be satisfactory in their probationary year when so many are perceived to teach unsatisfactory lessons?

Arguments based on statistical evidence need to be conducted with more circumspection than the anti-PGCE lobby have achieved. One thing seems clear though: the assertion that standards of teaching can be improved or even maintained by simply adopting an 'apprenticeship' model has no empirical support.

Apprenticeship and the development of sensibility

There is a central thesis in O'Hear's paper which is founded on a positive vision of teaching and learning (O'Hear, 1988). Following F R Leavis, he insists that all must begin from the 'training of sensibility'. Taking as his paradigm the realm of literature, O'Hear emphasizes 'the exercise of critical judgement, by considering the reactions of others to the work, by testing them against one's own reactions' (p 13). He goes on to portray learning as something like an apprenticeship and insists (following Polanyi) that the tacit, unspoken and judgemental aspects of the subject can only be communicated through this relationship (p 15). The art of teaching is certainly a complex, subtle and sensitive affair, hard to pin down with simple rules or to transmit merely through advice on methods. But this art cannot be learned only by imitation or through a totally tacit process. Even if teaching were essentially a set of psychomotor responses – much like driving a car – there would still be a need for structured instruction rather than simply learning by mistakes.

The 'apprentice' model of teacher education is inadequate for reasons given several years ago by John Wilson (Wilson, 1975). Wilson identifies three essential characteristics of the effective teacher: knowing one's subjects(s); being serious about, or caring for, the transmission of knowledge; understanding people. He then asks whether *copying* – the predominant mode of learning in apprenticeship – is really appropriate for the acquisition of these characteristics (p 131). Can we really copy someone's knowledge of a subject, his or her seriousness about learning or the quality of personal understanding? For this is what sensibility implies. Teaching is not just a set of identifiable skills but is bound up with knowledge, attitudes and understanding. Of course, an element of imitation may be present, but, as Wilson reminds us, what is copied may not always be desirable and 'experience' can be *bad* as well as good.

We should certainly not trust knowledge of a subject as the single criterion of teacher quality; indeed, by itself it can become a nuisance. As HMI tells us in *Teacher Training and the Secondary School*, (Department of Educational Science, 1981):

> The subject-centered approach is very deeply rooted, both in the students who enter BEd and PGCE and in the attitude of most of the schools where they will have their early experience as teachers. To break this circuit is no easy task (p 9).

Experience and educational theory

It is tempting and currently fashionable in Britain to take up an anti-intellectual stance and complain of theorizing, an activity which can be seen as remote from practicalities, in our case classrooms. But no human mind is free from the impulse towards theorizing, any more than human physiology can get by for long without breathing.

In his influential picture of the processes of human knowing, Karl Popper conceives of three distinct 'worlds' (Popper, 1972). The first of these is the world of physical states, of objects and observable events, the world we experience as 'out there'; the second is the world of mental states, the world we tend to regard as subjective experience; the third world is the world 'of theories in themselves, and their logical relations; of arguments in themselves; and of problem situations in themselves.' This last, 'World' is an autonomous world, it is a world of *ideas*, a world to which everyone contributes something but from which we all take much more. These ideas may take the form of scientific theories, philosophical reasonings, musical works, paintings, novels, poems, and so on.

All the inhabitants of '*World Three*' are the inevitable products of human thinking and imaginative speculation, inevitable in the same sense that spiders *must* make webs or birds *must* make nests. So we all make theories, seeking explanations, looking for organizing principles by which to have, to hold and to interpret experience, trying to formulate concepts that may have predictive power. If we did not, we would hardly survive from day to day. Lively and critical theorizing is one defence we have against the arbitrary, the subjective, the dogmatic and the doctrinaire; it is the way in which, as Popper says, we transcend ourselves.

Practical experience has to be assimilated, reflected upon, shared and refined. Professional development is in part the construction and perpetual adaptation of mutually shared networks of ideas. No profession can remain effective or accountable without debating key ideas or theories, bringing its assumptions out on to the table for public scrutiny.

Let us then resist theories that complain about theorizing as though it were an unnecessary waste of time. Secretaries of State for Education, DES inspectors, philosophers and teachers *all* theorize, well or badly as the case may be. One of the roles of schools and departments of education is to raise the standards of theorizing and to cultivate respect for and caution in handling the various types of evidence that bear upon educational transactions. This task may involve philosophical, psychological or sociological procedures or may be addressed to developing a clearer view of the nature of particular curriculum subjects. Much valuable work has been done in these intellectual areas in institutions where teachers are trained, or better, *educated*. A teacher who believes that education should be fundamentally child–centred, or someone who holds that a knowledge and love of a subject is the essential requirement for teaching effectiveness are both working to theories about children, the curriculum and educational processes. Theories are not the opposite of practice but its basis. Graduates embarking on PGCE courses already come with theories about education, sometimes unexamined in the form of prejudice. It is a major role of courses to examine these theories, though mostly in the practical context of teaching experience. Teaching is not simply a practical skill, nor can effectiveness be acquired by unthinking practice. We bring expectations and assumptions to teaching, theories about the subject and about the people we teach. These can serve either to illuminate or to confuse practice and they colour every action and judgement a teacher makes.

Notwithstanding this, criticism is still expressed about the inappropriateness of PGCE courses, assuming that they have a bias towards what is described as educational 'theory'. If analysis of classroom materials, the practice and discussion of teaching techniques, the sharing of professional perspective, the study of the social, psychological and administrative context of education are theoretical, then some departments of education are certainly guilty of this charge. Similarly, if we mean by theory the critical examination of assumptions, the sifting of evidence, the scrutiny of the operation of assessment procedures and other discourse about professional practice, then these are also frequently stated aims in teacher education. Any objective appraisal of the content of contemporary PGCE courses would find most of the time committed to curriculum subject work, much of this based in schools and aiming to assist in the development of effective and reflective teachers.

Of course, it can be argued that, ultimately, all depends on the individual teacher to find the magic spell that releases the spell of the subject and the energies of students. But we cannot rely totally on charismatic wizardry or on people picking up skills and positive attitudes by chance: we need to plan a little more for consistency of effectiveness and this planning is what teacher education is about. Most learning may indeed be tacit but this does not absolve us from consciously trying to find an optimum structure which helps to frame knowledge and organize experience:

> Experience-based courses need to be at least as carefully structured as those based on the orderly exposition of the theoretical elements of educational studies. It is not enough to put students into schools and expect that training will happen. They need training in observation (including observation while they are actually participating in teaching) and in interpreting what is observed (Department of Educational Science 1980).

Left to the inevitable and somewhat haphazard environment of schools, many students would flounder or give up, though some may hang on to become perpetually ineffective. Experience can desensitize as well as instruct. Our graduates deserve better than this: they need and value systematic help in the development of sensibility.

The views of PGCE students

In December, 1988, PGCE students at the Institute of Education, London University were given the following task:

> Please list briefly:
> Any professional help and support that you would have missed during the first term, had your training consisted *entirely* of experience in the school where you were on teaching practice (*without* Institute involvement).

In this way they were being indirectly asked to evaluate the feasibility of being 'apprentices', each student, as usual, being supported by and accountable to a designated member of the school staff for the duration of the practice period along the lines proposed by O'Hear and others. The request was put to them in the middle of the course, between two blocks of teaching practice. By this stage they had experienced two weeks of preliminary observation in schools and five weeks of block teaching practice plus several other school-based days along with their educational studies and curriculum courses.

This was not a quantitative but a qualitative small-scale study. Our essential concern was to identify the positive characteristics of one large PGCE course without prompting students or subjecting them to a replica of course-evaluation procedures. Responses were given anonymously, voluntarily and in confidence, and we would not wish to claim that this is a survey in the strict definition of that term. However, the evidence is important and does point to those valued qualities that distinguish the work of PGCE tutors and departments of education. Without coercion or reminders and at a very busy and stressful time of year, when students were out of the Institute in schools, around 10 per cent of those eligible to respond returned comments to us: 53 in all. Between them they contributed over 200 different items of comment most of which we were able to classify under 14 main headings. Curriculum course elements represented in the sample were: art and design, business studies, economics, English/drama, geography, history, mathematics, modern languages, music, religious education, science, social studies, and ESOL (English for Speakers of Other Languages). The following statements typify the views expressed; figures in brackets indicate the frequency of similar comments. Students would have missed:

The support of highly professional, skilled tutors (32)

'It is not enough just to read the recommended books; the ideas need to be discussed and worked on in the company of tutors who can guide and explain.'

'Institute tutors are knowledgeable, unbiased professionals, who are chosen for their experience and ability to share this with students.'

'The help, advice and support of people, who, although not currently school teachers, have a grasp of the subject-matter and teaching issues in one's particular field and who are not directly connected with the teaching-practice school.'

The sharing of ideas, experience and expertise with other students (35)

'I have learnt a great deal through interaction with fellow students, in particular through sharing ideas and debating issues.'

'Feeling that you are not entirely on your own.'

'PGCE students are able to share experiences, ideas and problems throughout the year.'

'We have support from other PGCE students – discovering that we all have the same hopes, fears, worries.'

'You need the time to debate with and learn from fellow PGCE students.'

An overview of the curriculum and a useful introduction to the whole area of assessment and testing (14)

'Would not have gained an overview of the curriculum and of the structure of its component parts.'

'Discussions have taken place on such major issues as the National Curriculum and assessment with informed educationalists.'

Discussion of key issues such as class, race, gender and special needs (19)

'Sound theoretical background and awareness of important issues like race, sex, class and special needs.'

'The course gave insight into such wider issues as sexism and racism.'

'Discussion of educational issues with wider social and political implications, eg: race and gender.'

Reading lists and access to an excellent library and media resources (27)

'Access to certain facilities such as the Institute library and the DEM.'

'The department of educational media and all its resources.'

Opportunity to reflect, evaluate, re-evaluate and analyse (10)

'Opportunity for reflection upon one's own aptitude for teaching; also the time to reflect upon methodology.'

'Opportunity to reflect, evaluate, re-evaluate and analyse; crucial for both professional and personal development which, for either to be successful, must go hand in hand.'

'Time to reflect on teaching outside the pressurized environment of secondary schools.'

'The need exists for a place and the time to reflect on and discuss (educational) practice and to relate it with theory for both specific examples and general issues.'

Ability to place the job of 'teacher' within a clear framework (7)

'The theoretical framework promotes the idea that teaching is a profession.'

'The PGCE year places the job of 'teacher' within a clear framework, theoretically and practically.'

Help with lesson preparation (15)

'Guidance on lesson planning and preparation.'

'The ability to acquire confidence in planning lesson content: practical hints for transferring ideas into workable plans.'

'Approaches to the classroom: discussion of applicability of course materials, etc.'

Systematic help with teaching skills and classroom control (14)

As opposed to 'tips for teachers' or 'off-the-cuff pedagogy.'

'Strategies for handling classroom conflict.'

Professional contacts with teachers in various schools (7)

'Visits to meet teachers in other schools: the introduction to the school situation within the security of your own group.'

'Each school seems so different, it is very valuable to share ideas with

other teachers and students.'
'The opportunity to discuss and review the quality of individual schools
objectively.'

Discussion of recent work on child development (5)

'Tutors are experts in their field – the information they give is
very up to date, eg: theories of reading and writing and child
development.'
'Provision of an overview in curriculum subjects and child development.'

Experience in a single school would be restrictive (3)

Such experience would be 'limited', 'unbalanced', 'narrow', 'biased'.
Teachers would become 'de-skilled', 'de-professionalized' if their
training consisted entirely of experience in their teaching practice
schools.

Without the support of the Institute, students would have felt isolated and disturbed (5)

'You walk into a classroom for the first time shell-shocked enough;
if there was nothing to call on but a rather spurious notion of
"commonsense", would we ever go back?'
'To have been placed in a TP school in isolation for the full duration of
the course would have been frightening and demoralizing, and I doubt
if I would have lasted the course.'

Despite a willingness to be helpful, most teachers in schools would lack the time and energy to give adequate support to apprentices (11)

'Institute tutors provide valuable support in the form of advice and
time. It is evident that full-time teachers are not able to do this
adequately.'
'PGCE students are still students, and need strong support and guidance
– not available in overworked and understaffed schools.'
'Unfortunately, in schools there seem to be many teachers whose
depression and frustration at their working conditions, etc, could easily
put the student off for life.'
'Fully qualified teachers in schools are so pushed for time and energy,
they can give little support/advice "on the job".'
'Professional support is just not available from often overworked
teaching colleagues.'

Some further comments:

'I consider that the professional guidance and support throughout the first term have been invaluable and of the highest quality: a large and vital part of my development as a teacher.'

'To learn through experience alone could mean to damage children through your own mistakes.'

'Education is not solely about experience; education is about opening up horizons and trying to aid people to break out of their narrow canyons. The Institute is the place where we are challenged.'

Clearly, the discussion of real and important educational issues, appraisal of available materials, access to more than one school, expert support and familiarity with a wide range of practical ideas and materials are among the special and valued functions of departments of education; promoting a sense of objectivity towards a complex and demanding task. Teacher education has as its aims exactly those qualities looked for by Professor O'Hear – 'training in sensitivity' and 'the development of critical judgement'. Teaching is not a mindless activity and many of our our best young graduates are not going to be persuaded otherwise. Nor are they convinced that these virtues are best promoted merely by classroom experience or that schools as they are presently staffed and funded could achieve these aims. Two more responses make this clear.

In any one-year professional course with a necessarily high proportion of practical experience [teaching practice], the need exists for a place and the time to reflect on and discuss practice and to relate it with the theory for both specific examples and general issues. A PGCE course conducted solely in schools and FE colleges would not allow this; the professional support is just not available from overworked teaching colleagues.

'Without PGCE, [I] would not ever have considered taking teaching as a profession; without sound training leading to a hard-worked-for qualification, education itself becomes devalued, deprofessionalised and deskilled.'

One able PGCE student (now in post) completed a successful and rewarding teaching practice in a very supportive school where there were excellent role models and confidence among the teachers that they could handle a large part of teacher training. Even so, she wrote to me saying 'it would have been a disaster if I had done my training based only in school – I don't think I would have lasted.'

Summary of responses:

Students valued the PGCE because it provides for:

- the support of highly professional, skilled tutors;
- the sharing of ideas, experience and expertise with other students;
- an overview of the curriculum and a useful introduction to the whole area of assessment and testing;
- discussion of key issues in education, such as class, race, gender and special needs;
- reading lists and access to an excellent library and media resources;
- the opportunity to reflect, evaluate, re-evaluate and analyse;
- the ability to place the job of 'teacher' within a clear framework;
- help with lesson preparation;
- systematic help with teaching skills and classroom control;
- professional contacts with teachers in various schools;
- discussion of recent work on child development;

If the course were not available students thought that:

- experience in a single school would be restrictive/limited/un-balanced/narrow/biased;
- without the support of the Institute, students would have felt isolated and disturbed;
- despite a willingness to be helpful, most teachers in schools would lack the time and energy to give adequate support to 'apprentices'.

Clearly, these student teachers do not have great confidence in any form of training based in a single school. Nor do they see a PGCE as a waste of time. Teachers in schools are not perceived to have the time and energy to devote to the development of 'sensibility'.

The 1988 HMI survey of initial teacher training in universities (Department of Education on Science, 1988a) points out:

With very few exceptions, students on initial training courses work with enthusiasm, challenging and stimulating their pupils and their tutors. They generally respond well when high standards are set: nearly all show signs of becoming competent teachers and some are exceptionally able (p 43).

What then happens to these student teachers? Why the negative reports from the HMI when it comes down to the job itself? The answer may have to do with the inevitable strain of the first year of teaching, the quality of this 'experience' and the patchy support given to many of these lively young people in their first posts.

It is very easy to forget how difficult and complex teaching is and how much there is to learn and become sensitive to. The issue of how far teachers in schools can undertake a substantial part of this work therefore needs approaching realistically. Even if it were considered to be generally desirable, feasibility would need to be demonstrated. There are reasons to suppose that new teachers are not always adequately supported during their probationary year. Can we then be certain that they might be properly supervised during initial training if this were to become even more school-based?

The perceptions of teachers

A questionnaire was sent to all teachers having responsibility for students in over 500 primary and secondary schools where students were placed on teaching practice from the Institute of Education during the academic year 1988–1989. The first 198 of the returns were analysed; 22 from primary, 169 from secondary, four from sixth-form colleges, one from a sixth-form centre and two from tertiary colleges. Three of the 198 were private schools. School size ranged from the smallest primary, with 150 on roll, to a secondary of over 2,000: altogether very representative of the range of British schools.

Although five of the teachers had not had previous experience of supervising students, most were experienced in this role and two-thirds had worked with students for five years or more. The following table shows the status of those involved in student supervision.

One intention in this study was to gauge the extent to which teachers saw students as prepared for teaching practice. Table 6.2 gives the

Primary	
Head	1
Deputy	2
Class teacher	19
Secondary	
Deputy	23
Senior teacher	6
INSET co-ord	1
Head faculty	7
Head of dept	131
Main scale	1
Other	
Vice principal	2
Head of dept	7

Table 6.1 *Total number of teacher supervisors surveyed*

	Primary	Secondary	Other
Well-prepared (46%)	9	74	2
Fairly well-prepared (44%)	12	68	2
Inadequately prepared (10%)	1	17	1

(n=188: 10 incomplete responses were discounted.)

Table 6.2 *How teachers perceive student preparedness*

figures. Only 10 per cent of students were perceived to be inadequately prepared, – not ideal perhaps but certainly no disgrace when compared with the outstandingly favourable impression.

Table 6.3 shows the perceived levels of dependency on school staff. From these we might notice that *on their own estimation* over a quarter of the teachers hardly ever gave basic ideas for lessons while 38 per cent thought they hardly ever advised on detailed lesson-planning. About a quarter, on their own account, gave little help with class management. One-third rarely helped with the organization of materials. Substantial involvement in these elements of training appears to be fairly rare, even though it seems that they might be best handled in the school setting.

The vast majority of these teachers agree with PGCE students that they just do not have the time or other resources adequately to undertake the major training responsibility in addition to the manifold and increasing demands upon them *as teachers*. One hundred and fifty of the 198 said that this was not possible – against 46 who thought it was and two who were not sure. Time, other commitments, responsibility in the first instance to pupils, along with lack of training and resources are all given as reasons for a negative response. They see a positive role for the college-based part of the PGCE. The most frequently mentioned elements of the university's function include: innovations and ideas; planning teaching sequences and curriculum development, including the National Curriculum; objectivity and academic study including theory of education; an overview and varied practice; child development and psychology; assessment; an orientation into the profession; research awareness.

There were many comments about the difficulties of a totally school-based training. One teacher suggested that it was very important to have an 'overview of education offered *without prejudice* (school-based teachers can become cynical and may be a negative influence).' Another warned that

(P = Primary; S = Secondary; O = Other)

| | Substantially | | | To some extent | | | Hardly ever | | |
	P	S	O	P	S	O	P	S	O
Basic ideas for lessons (26%)	2	38	2 (21%)	11	88	4 (52%)	9	43	0
Detailed lesson planning (38%)	3	46	2 (26%)	8	61	1 (35%)	11	62	3
Sequencing lessons (24%)	3	56	2 (31%)	11	75	2 (44%)	8	38	2
Feedback on lessons (23%)	4	59	1 (32%)	11	74	3 (44%)	7	36	2
Organizing materials (33%)	6	49	2 (29%)	10	62	2 (36%)	6	58	2
Class management (24%)	6	44	2 (26%)	11	84	2 (49%)	5	41	2

Table 6.3 *Perceived levels of dependency on teachers*

school-based training would, in many instances, provide no variety of experience, no understanding, no support for problems, no proper curriculum-continuity vision. It would produce inflexible, stressed, inadequate teachers who would probably drop out or, worse, be incapable of improving.

Even when teachers do express confidence over their role as teacher educators, this does not necessarily mean that students in their charge always share this perception. We have already drawn attention to one instance where a highly experienced teacher felt very confident of handling most elements of initial teacher education but where the student in the school was emphatic in expressing a need for the wider perspective of a structured course and experience of other schools; a view reinforced by her further experience throughout the rest of the PGCE year.

Conclusion

There is little if any substance to the arguments against the effectiveness of PGCE courses. An uncritical use of statistics coupled with a naive and simplistic view of the job of teaching may have a popular following but is hopelessly inadequate as a basis for evaluating professional preparation. The acute problem of teacher shortages will not be met by taking in the uneducated. Some will just be poor teachers finding an easy way to get into the profession without careful scrutiny, while others will default without the mediation and support of education departments. Worst of all, the profession will begin to lose its cutting edge if systematically deprived of opportunities for critical reflection, self-evaluation and the extension of perspectives beyond the confines of one classroom. Nor can this opportunity be deferred to in-service study after some years' experience. By then the profession will have lost too many teachers. In any case, most INSET is currently organized and carried out piecemeal in LEA's and eventually under the uncertainties of Local Management of Schools. The chance to participate in more substantial courses has been greatly eroded. Regrettable and short-sighted as this might be, the fact does emphasize the need to make initial teacher education as effective as possible and to ensure that the PGCE route into the profession is followed by all but an exceptionally well qualified small minority.

Systematic help with teaching skills; redefining curriculum subjects in more relevant and intercultural ways; setting the social and psychological context of educational transactions; giving dependable professional and personal support and encouraging critical thinking against a background of broad and structured school experience: these are the key functions of the PGCE. The present irony is that on the one hand the PGCE is thought by some to be unnecessary and on the other hand it becomes increasingly constrained by a structure and content largely determined by agencies having little direct knowledge either of classrooms or of training for them. The latest novelty to be externally imposed is the Enterprise and Education Initiative Project, introducing into teacher education 'awareness of the needs of business and industry'.

The 1989 *Criteria for the Approval of Initial Teacher Training Courses*, (Department of Education and Science, 1989 dc), imposes yet more imperatives on course planners and tutors, though often specifying what is already in hand. The list is long: an understanding of the way in which pupils develop and learn; organizing work as a progression; the capacity to use a range of teaching methods; the ability to identify gifted pupils and those with special needs; skills in testing and assessment; guarding against preconceptions based on race and gender; the ability to teach controversial subjects in a balanced way; group-management techniques; information technology; pastoral and legal responsibilities; links with parents and communities; the social context of schools; planning schemes of work; the ability to plan, assess and provide advice to others on subject content; extending subject knowledge; and so on and so on. All this and more is required to be explicitly brought about by training establishments. Oddly though, very little is said about the specific teaching role of schools and teachers in schools. Is it perhaps assumed that school experience per se is bound to be effective without designated resources, a declared structure and a set of criteria by which it can be evaluated? If so, this goes against first-hand evidence.

It is time that those responsible for initial teacher education were adequately facilitated to get on with the job of developing courses in close collaboration with teachers working in schools. The articled teacher scheme may be a step forward here. Further progress will need a properly costed resource basis. Meanwhile, we must be watchful of those well away from schools and classrooms who think they know best. This knowledge often seems based on a shaky reading of DES statistics and on unrealistic and outdated views of the PGCE, possibly coloured by a childhood perception of teaching being easy and uncomplicated.

Chapter 7

The Control of Teacher Education: The Council for the Accreditation of Teacher Education

William Taylor

Introduction

In all countries, official concern with the training and supply of an adequate number of teachers to staff the nation's schools has gone hand in hand with the development of state-supported education. Sometimes – as in England and Wales in the nineteenth century – the task has been entrusted to the churches or other voluntary bodies. Elsewhere, and at other times, the role of the state has been limited to control of numbers and recognition of end-of-course examinations for the award of qualified-teacher status, leaving course design and content to the institutions. In England and Wales, as elsewhere, responsibility for granting qualified-teacher status to those who complete approved courses of training, rests with the Secretaries of State for Education and Science.

The institutes of education created to coordinate teacher education after the Second World War (all, except Cambridge, university-based and funded) were recognized in official regulations as Area Training Organizations (ATOs) competent to approve courses of training, the graduates of which would receive qualified-teacher status in addition to the certification degree awarded by their university (or, later the Council for National Academic Awards (CNAA).

With the abrogation of the separate training-of-teachers regulations in 1975, responsibility for the academic award and for professional recognition was separated. Academic validation remained the province of the chartered bodies, namely the universities and, for the polytechnics and colleges of higher education, the CNNA. Without the ATOs to turn to for advice on professional recognition, the Secretary of State for Education and Science established local professional committees which, although their constitutions and membership required official approval, developed on a largely bottom-up and ad hoc basis. These were always regarded as an interim measure prior to new national machinery being set up to make recommendations on the professional approval of initial-teacher-training courses to the Secretary of State.

It was not, however, until 1984 that the Council for the Accreditation of Teacher Education (CATE) came into being, with a five-year remit. In November 1989 the Secretary of State announced that CATE would continue in operation for a further period, with extended terms of reference. The remainder of this chapter sets out the background to CATE's establishment and how its initial remit was discharged, together with an outline of its future tasks.

Background

Between the early seventies and eighties, teacher education in England and Wales underwent radical changes in structure, in organization and in control. The setting up of CATE has to be seen in the context of these changes.

At the beginning of the 1970s, teacher education was undertaken by some 160 self-standing, single-purpose colleges of education, by a number of the 30 polytechnics that had been created in the mid sixties, and by some 20 university departments of education.

The colleges and polytechnics offered three-year certificate in education and three- and four-year bachelor of education courses for aspiring primary and secondary teachers. Most of the one-year Postgraduate Certificate in Education (PGCE) programmes for candidates for secondary teaching who already had a university degree in arts or science were provided by departments of education in universities, which also offered a variety of in-service and advanced courses for serving teachers and undertook research.

The certificates and degrees for which the colleges taught were those of the universities they were associated with through university-based ATOs set up as a means of coordinating initial teacher education in the years following the McNair report on teacher training at the end of the Second World War.

Demographic downturn leading to diminished demand for teachers, financial exigency and the reorganization of non-university higher education, led during the seventies to the virtual disappearance of single-purpose colleges of education in England and Wales. Some joined existing polytechnics. Others combined forces or linked with further-education colleges to form new multipurpose colleges and institutes of higher education. A few merged with universities. Several were closed and their buildings sold or used for other educational purposes.

This reorganization had important consequences for the university connection forged during the post-war years by means of the ATO arrangements, and for the way in which degrees and certificates for teachers received academic and professional approval.

Some of the former colleges of education continued to teach for the awards of the universities with which they had been associated, or in a few cases those of other universities. The polytechnics and most of the new colleges and institutes of higher education sought academic validation from the CNAA, set up in the sixties to offer opportunities for non-university institutions to teach for university-standard degrees.

In addition to linking teacher-training institutions with the universities that conferred their degrees and certificates, the ATOs had also made recommendations to the Secretary of State for Education and Science for conferment of qualified-teacher status. The professional committees of the ATOs, on which sat representatives of the local employing authorities and of the teachers, were also an important source of advice on the structure and content of teacher-training programmes.

The withdrawal of the teacher-training regulations that accompanied the disappearance of colleges of education as a separate sector of post-secondary provision entailed the disappearance of the ATOs. Who should now advise the Secretary of State on professional accreditation?

Although interim regional professional committees were set up in 1975, it was not until nine years later that national arrangements were agreed. In April 1984 the establishment of CATE was announced 'to advise the Secretaries of State for Education and Science on the approval of initial-teacher-training courses in England and Wales.'

Context

The setting up of CATE reflected not only a gap in the arrangements for the approval of initial training courses in England and Wales, but a worldwide concern about the content and quality of teacher preparation. In the United States, in Europe, in Australia, New Zealand, Canada and other economically advanced countries, the seventies saw a series of reports on the needs and shortcomings of teacher preparation which shared many common features.

Teacher educators were no strangers to criticism. In many countries, their task had for a long time been identified with preparing those who would work in the lower schools – elementary, primary and non-selective secondary. As such, teacher education had been more a part of secondary than of higher education. To train for teaching had been an avenue of limited social mobility for the sons and daughters of the upwardly mobile working class, rather than a royal road to worldly success. The status and rewards of teaching had not been able to compete with those of other occupations for the attention of the most talented.

Lacking an efficient technology and clearly definable production function, teaching had been vulnerable to the attacks of those who had chosen to stress the weaknesses and the failures, rather than the strengths and the successes, of mass education. In many countries, there could still be found those who maintained that the only training teachers needed was effective induction into an academic discipline, plus a spot of apprenticeship.

All this had been familiar enough. Those in the trade had learned to live with it. But the criticism that really began to count in the seventies was much more sharply focused on the process and content of teacher education itself, rather than its alleged educational and social characteristics.

It was suggested that insufficient care had been taken to ensure that candidates for teacher training were adequately motivated and had personalities appropriate to teaching; that the courses they followed lacked academic and professional coherence; that the subject content of these courses was not always at a level adequate to higher education, or properly related to students' professional studies; that both subject and professional studies were not sufficiently geared to the particular needs of schools of the kind in which students would subsequently work; that many teacher–education staff did not have experience relevant to their tasks; that the practical work in schools that formed part of the course was not always well timed or organized; and that practising teachers were insufficiently involved in the selection of students, the design of programmes, the teaching of courses and the assessment of performance.

In England and Wales, where there were no national prescriptions about the structure and content of training programmes, it was also argued that since qualified–teacher status conferred the right to teach in any primary or secondary school in which a teacher could obtain an appointment, variations in time devoted to different aspects of the training course in different institutions – from 13 to 50 per cent in the case of subject studies, for example – were unacceptable.

Discussion of teacher education has long been dominated by questions of numbers and supply – persistent shortages during the sixties being followed by the institutional consequences of contraction during the early seventies. During the second half of the decade more time began to be devoted to organization and content. Governments, industrialists and trade unionists all showed concern for the part that education might play in overcoming skill shortages, benefiting international competitiveness, enhancing personal adaptability within rapidly changing markets for labour, rectifying unfavourable attitudes towards industry and manufacture, and improving productivity.

In all this, teachers were seen to have an important part to play. Fresh interest began to be shown in their recruitment, selection, initial preparation, appointment, induction and in-service and advanced training. Her Majesty's Inspectorate (HMI) produced papers for discussion by the government's Advisory Committee on the Supply and Education of Teachers (ACSET), a representative body first appointed in 1973 (as the Advisory Committee on the Supply and Training of Teachers (ACSTT)), as well as reports on aspects of the teacher-preparation process, and on the deployment of qualified teachers by schools.

As a result of discussions within ACSET and with professional interest groups such as the Universities Council for the Education of Teachers (UCET), agreement emerged that responsibility for making recommendations to the Secretary of State on the acceptability of initial-teacher-training courses for the award of qualified-teacher status should be that of a new national body, rather than of regional organizations.

The context in which such national bodies were established had changed greatly from the 1960s. Governments were placing greater emphasis on the efficient use of public resources, and were anxious about the effects of single-interest politics on the work of advisory bodies. Education had become a field of contested values. It was not easy to obtain unequivocal agreement to what constituted the public interest. In our post-Freudian, iconoclastic age, claims of disinterestedness on the part of any one group tend to evoke a sceptical response. One of the costs of democratization is the demand that representatives be accountable to their own constituencies. There is consequent difficulty in achieving consensus. The number of organizations that might claim to be represented on a body concerned with a subject such as teacher education is large.

As a consequence of all this there has been reluctance to constitute new advisory and quasi-governmental bodies on strictly representational principles, and a preference to leave nominations, after appropriate consultation, to the Secretary of State. At the same time, reflecting constraints on public resources, new bodies have initially been funded at modest levels and given relatively short time horizons for their tasks. Any resources that institutions must deploy as a consequence of the activities of such bodies are now normally to be obtained from within budget savings rather than by the injection of new money.

The statutory position

All these considerations helped to shape the organization and remit of CATE between 1984 and 1989. Its powers derived from a government circular issued in April 1984 (3/84) which, for the first time, laid down the criteria that courses were required to meet in order to receive professional approval and for their graduates to be granted qualified-teacher status (Department of Education on Science, 1984).

The criteria, some aspects of which stimulated lively debate and are further discussed below, deal with the selection of students, qualifications and experience of staff, organization of courses, balance of subject studies and subject method, educational and professional studies, and assessment and certification. It has to be emphasized that CATE's duties were in respect of professional accreditation. Academic validation remained a responsibility of the CNAA and of individual universities. There were in practice three distinct but related processes of control involved in providing courses of initial teacher training.

First, in the case of universities, the University Grants Committee (UGC) had to share out among individual institutions the total initial-teacher-training intake places allocated to the university sector by the Secretary of State. In the case of polytechnics and colleges, the Secretary of State had the formal powers of allocation, on advice (for parts of the period with which we are concerned) from the National Advisory Body for Public Sector Higher Education (NAB) or its Welsh counterpart. This process is known as administrative course approval.

Secondly, the CNAA or a validating university had to agree that a course met appropriate standards leading to an academic award. This process is usually referred to as validation. The CNNA or university judgements relate to the academic standards of the whole course, including its professional aspects.

Thirdly, under schedule 5 of the Education (Teachers) Regulations Act 1982, the Secretary of State was responsible for approving the course as being suitable for the professional preparation of teachers and hence for the award of qualified-teacher status on successful completion. It was the task of CATE to advise the Secretary of State on the exercise of this power; this is the process of professional accreditation.

The distinctions between these different kinds of approval are of great importance. One of the reasons why interim arrangements for professional approval introduced after the demise of the ATOs in 1975 were unsatisfactory was lack of clarity in the relation between academic validation and professional recognition. As far as the former Certificate in Education had been concerned, both functions had been within the remit of the ATOs. When the Bachelor of Education degree was introduced in the late 1960s, at first for only a small proportion of college students, university departments and faculties other than education began to be involved. Under the post-1975 interim arrangements, the CNAA designated its Committee for Teacher Education, which oversaw the academic validation of courses, as the committee responsible for making recommendations to the Secretary of State on professional recognition.

It has been argued that the validating and professional-recognition aspects of teacher education should be 'fully integrated'. Given the statutory background, it is difficult to see what this means. Integrating the academic and professional content of a course is one thing and is essentially a matter for validating bodies – CNNA or universities. Integrating academic validation and professional approval is quite another. To do so either denies universities and the CNAA the academic autonomy that is properly theirs, or fails to recognize the Secretary of State's statutory responsibilities.

ACSET stated the position clearly in advice to the Secretary of State in August 1983 which led to the establishment of CATE:

> We see validation as properly concerned with all those aspects of a course which bear on the decision by the validating university or the CNAA to award degrees on successful completion. Such consideration of 'degree worthiness' should entail assessment of the course as a whole – ie, its professional aspects as well as academic content and standard. Similarly, we would expect the Secretary of State to have an interest in all those aspects of the course which bear on the judgement about its suitability as a professional preparation for teaching. His consideration would not be limited to the 'professional' or practical teaching aspects, but would extend also to questions involving academic content and standard. We see validation and accreditation as complementary processes. Each concerned properly with the whole course, but arising from quite separate sources of authority – university and CNAA charters as regards validation, the Secretary of State's formal approval powers as regards accreditation (Advisory Committee on the supply and Education of Teachers, 1983).

When distinct but interrelated judgements, recommendations, and decisions about the work of single institutions have to be taken by a number of separate bodies, clear definitions of function are needed if confusion is to be avoided. And there must also be an appropriate sequence of action.

CATE – structure and procedures

The membership of CATE was settled, and the Council held its first meeting, in the early Autumn of 1984. The original members were all nominated by the Secretary of State after consultation with relevant organizations. Four were serving teachers, two from secondary and two from primary/middle schools. Four came from local education authorities (the employers of teachers in England and Wales), two of these being chief education officers and two elected members of authorities. Three members were in public-sector institutions which undertook initial teacher training. Another three were from universities, one of whom worked in a university department of education. One member was the general secretary of one of the national teachers' associations, two were senior industrialists, and there was one local-education-authority chief inspector and one educational journalist. The Chief Inspector (HMI) for Teacher Education, and other senior HMI personnel and officers of the Department of Education and Science acted as assessors. Later, when CATE was given responsibility for making recommendations in respect of initial-teacher-education courses in Northern Ireland, a member and assessor from that province were added.

Several members of CATE fell into more than one category. One of the teacher members, for example, was past-president of the country's largest teachers' organization. One of the local-authority-elected members was also a deputy headmaster in another authority. Two of the teacher members came from Wales. But it has again to be emphasized that members were not appointed in a representative capacity. All served in their own right, and gave about three days each month to attending CATE meetings in addition to the time needed to study the extensive documentation that institutions and the CATE secretariat produced as part of the review process.

CATE was served by a full-time secretariat of four, seconded by the Department of Education and Science but with self-contained offices in Elizabeth House.

Initial teacher training is currently provided by some 90 institutions – universities, polytechnics and colleges – in England and Wales and Northern Ireland. CATE was concerned with the accreditation of individual courses, not that of institutions. Circular 3/84 suggested that the first review should be completed within 'three to four years'. In the event, over five years were required.

CATE did not begin the review of an institution's courses until a detailed report by HMI on the institution's initial-teacher-training provision was available. These reports resulted from HMI team inspections in each institution. In the case of polytechnics and colleges

HMI reports are published by the Department of Education and Science. Inspectors also visited university departments of education by invitation. The subsequent report was sent to the university concerned, which decided for itself whether or not to publish; several did so.

Institutions were asked by CATE to provide detailed information about their courses, the qualifications and experience of their staff and other matters relevant to the published accreditation criteria.

All this material was considered by one of CATE's three reporting groups, which also met institutional representatives in London to elucidate particular points and, occasionally, paid local visits.

Reporting groups made proposals of four kinds to meetings of the full Council:

1. If all relevant criteria were satisfied, a proposal would be made to recommend to the Secretary of State the approval of the course under schedule 5 of the regulations.

2. If there was still work to be done to satisfy certain criteria and it appeared that this would be achieved within a reasonable period, the group would propose that a recommendation for schedule-5 approval be made conditional upon further progress within a specified timetable.

3. Where it was clear that a great deal remained to be done before the criteria were satisfied, the group would propose that no recommendation be made but that the matter be reconsidered after a further period of, say, 12 months.

4. There were cases where even after reconsideration a positive recommendation could not be proposed and the reporting group suggested that the Council recommend to the Secretary of State that approval be withheld or withdrawn.

CATE made known to the institutions concerned, its recommendations to the Secretary of State and the fact that they had been made to the UGC and the NAB. When the Secretary of State had considered the matter and reached a decision, this was published by the Department of Education and Science.

Problems and issues

During the first 18 months of CATE's operation a number of aspects of the criteria and of the review process attracted particular comment from within sectors of the teacher-education community. Of these, the most prominent was the requirement in respect of subject study for the three- and four-year Bachelor of Education degree. The criteria had this to say on the matter:

> The higher education and initial teacher training of all intending teachers should include the equivalent of at least two full years' course time devoted to subject studies at a level appropriate to higher education. In BEd courses for the primary years, a wide area of the curriculum might constitute the student's specialism and the time allocated to this part of the course should include the application of the subjects concerned to the learning and developmental needs of young children. In BEd courses for secondary teaching, the two years should be spent in the study of one or two subjects within the secondary curriculum as it is at present or as it may be expected to develop in the foreseeable future (Department of Education and Science, 1984, p 7).

The criteria also embodied requirements that courses include adequate attention to the methodology of teaching the chosen subject specialism or curricular area, that primary students should in addition devote about 100 hours to studying the teaching of mathematics and similar time to the teaching of language, and that 'the professional studies of intending primary teachers should, moreover, prepare them for their wider role of class teacher . . .'.

Debates about the respective place of subject studies and other elements in courses of initial training are of long standing. In the nineteenth century (and, in some systems, well into the twentieth), many teacher-training students had not completed a full secondary education. What were known as 'main subject' studies were intended to compensate for their lack of both depth and breadth.

During the sixties, anxieties about the quality of teachers entering primary schools led the influential Plowden Report on Primary Education to state:

> The content of the course varies both between institutes and between individual colleges, but there is much common ground. All students undertake an advanced study of one or two subjects (main courses). Some teachers question whether this is necessary for students training to be primary-school teachers. We accept the general view that study in some depth forms an essential part of the education of any teacher. The practising teacher will be learning to be a teacher all his life but he may have less opportunity, once he leaves college, for the systematic study of a subject for its own sake. Students need resources of knowledge and judgement upon which they can draw

both as teachers and as individuals, and these will not necessarily be related to the day-to-day work of primary schools. We are advised that there is wide variation in the standards attained by students in their main courses. The best already reach the level of an ordinary degree, but at the other end of the scale are students who pass at a level little beyond the advanced level in the GCE examination (Department of Education and Science, 1967, p 344, para 972)

Discussion during this period of what constituted the most appropriate curriculum for future primary teachers was also influenced by differences in the basis of recruitment of staff to the education and subject departments in the colleges, and by the academic requirements of validating bodies concerning the new BEd degree. Specialists in the college subject departments had been recruited mainly from grammar and selective schools, while an increasing number of education-department staff were people with good primary or secondary modern experience, and advanced qualifications in one of the disciplines of education, rather than in academic subjects.

HMI reports on aspects of primary education during the seventies indicated weaknesses in teachers' subject knowledge and identified the gains that came from members of staff being able to make a specialist or semi-specialist contribution as a member of the primary teaching team. This came out clearly in the HMI Primary Survey of 1978:

> Students preparing to teach in primary schools require opportunities to exploit their academic strengths and to convert them in ways that will enable them to contribute in a specialist sense in a primary school. This presupposes the ability to initiate and implement programmes of work in the teachers' own area of expertise and to advise and help other teachers who may have different strengths (Department of Education and Science, 1978, pp 122–3).

This view was repeated in the paper on the content of initial teacher education that HMI prepared for ACSET discussion in 1982, which went on to say that:

> It therefore follows that all BEd students preparing for the primary phase should follow one curriculum area in some depth, following an appropriate A-level success or its equivalent, which occupies the equivalent of two full years of the undergraduate course. (Department of Education and Science, 1983, p. 5)

This view was incorporated in the criteria which formed the basis of CATE reviews. It continued to occasion comment from teacher educators committed to alternative forms of course organization, in which subject and professional studies were closely integrated.

Prominent among other criteria which attracted attention within and beyond the teacher-education profession was the requirement that teacher-education staff concerned with pedagogy should have 'enjoyed recent success as teachers of the age range to which their training courses are directed, and should maintain regular and frequent experience of classroom teaching.'

The rapid contraction of teacher education in the seventies made it difficult for colleges and departments to maintain an adequate rate of recruitment of experienced staff from the schools. Steps are now being taken to rectify such shortages. Where this criterion could not be rapidly satisfied, the circular suggested that employing institutions should provide opportunities for staff to 'demonstrate their effectiveness in schools, for example by means of secondments to schools or schemes for tutor/schoolteacher exchanges.' In the course of its reviews CATE looked for the existence within an institution of a systematic staff-development plan whereby these criteria could be met and for evidence of close links between training institutions and schools.

Impact and evaluation

In its five years of operation under Circular 3/84, CATE held 44 full Council meetings, and its reporting groups met on more than 330 occasions. During the Council's first year, positive recommendations were made to the Secretary of State in respect of only half the courses reviewed. In 1986 this proportion rose to two out of three, and in 1987/88 to five out of six.

Prominent among the reasons that led to the rejection of courses in the early stages of the Council's work were deficiencies in the quantity and quality of subject studies; inadequate provision for studying the teaching of such subjects in classroom settings; lack of recent and relevant experience on the part of staff concerned with pedagogy; insufficiently comprehensive staff-development programmes; weaknesses in local committee arrangements; too little involvement in selection and course planning by experienced teachers; inappropriate balances between contact and private study time within the 100 hours of mathematics and language study required of intending primary teachers; poor coverage of the elements of educational and professional study demanded by the criteria; and inadequate curriculum-studies provision in primary courses.

Between 1984 and 1989 the majority of institutions were able to rectify most of these weaknesses, although right up to the end of CATE's first remit, there were still instances of subjects being presented for approval that were inappropriate to the curriculum of the primary school –

especially in the context of the National Curriculum legislated for in the 1988 Education Reform Act. Some other familiar deficiencies continued to recur, and in addition, new issues arose from the introduction of the extended PGCE for experienced non-graduates in shortage subjects, the increased proportion of entrants with non-standard qualifications to certain courses, and other innovatory schemes intended to broaden the basis of entry to teaching.

While CATE was at work, HMI continued to survey the state of teacher preparation and to publish their findings, in particular in a further survey of beginning teachers – *The New Teacher in School (1987)* (Department of Education and Science, 1988c) – and in the Report of the Senior Chief Inspector (SCI) – *Standards in Education, 1987–88* (Department of Education and Science, 1989a). The SCI found considerable changes for the better in initial teacher education, including improved balance between theory and practice; a higher proportion of staff with recent and relevant experience of teaching in schools; better links between institutional and school-based work; more effective partnerships between institutions and schools; improved academic rigour in courses; a clear subject/curriculum match and evidence that ITT students 'respond confidently and enthusiastically to demands made of them'. A year later, in February 1990, the SCI's report found that

In general the quality of the ITT courses inspected was good. . . . The general picture is encouraging. Institutions continue to respond constructively to the Secretary of State's criteria for further education, and the work of the CATE. In particular, institutions are improving staff development, most importantly by including opportunities for lecturers to work in schools (Department of Education and Science, 1990, paras 104–5, p 17).

On the other hand, some of the weaknesses identified in the *New Teacher in School* persisted, including lack of sufficient preparation in the organization and management of learning; poor assessment and recording of pupil progress, an undeveloped understanding of ways in which children learn and develop; and problems in dealing with different levels of ability.

The reconstituted Council

The original remit of the Council for the Accreditation of Teacher Education, having been renewed for a year, was due to expire at the end of 1989. In the middle of that year, the Secretary of State issued a consultation document proposing that CATE be reconstituted with somewhat different terms of reference. In the light of the large number of comments and suggestions received, the draft criteria and the accompanying commentary were revised and new Circulars (24/89, Welsh Office Circular 59/89, Northern Ireland Circular 1989/40) were issued (Department of Education and Science, 1989b).

The consultation process had revealed substantial support for continuation of CATE's work, not least from within the teacher-education community. This was in contrast to attitudes expressed five years earlier. CATE's implementation of the Circular 3/84 criteria, especially those relating to subject studies and recent and relevant experience, had initially occasioned a great deal of anxiety and not a little hostility, particularly from those concerned with preparing teachers for primary schools. During the five years of its existence, CATE had worked hard to demonstrate that the purpose of the criteria was not to specify what constitutes an acceptable course, but to establish certain minimum requirements that any good programme should satisfy. It was not CATE's purpose to impose a single model of teacher education. The experience of 1984–89 showed that satisfying the criteria did not preclude a great variety of approaches to course design and execution.

In the five years in which CATE operated under the terms of Circular 3/84, representatives from every teacher-preparing institution in England, Wales and Northern Ireland met the reporting-group teams concerned with their submissions. Local committees operated throughout the country. Although as national conferences organized by CATE showed, many of their chairpersons and members would have liked a better definition of their role, especially once approval by the Secretary of State of the courses for which they had provided support had been secured.

The introduction of arrangements whereby mature men and women with suitable experience and educational records could be employed as 'licensed teachers' and subsequently recommended by employing authorities for qualified status; the start-up of the school-based articled-teachers scheme, and continued evidence of dissatisfaction on the part of some politicians and commentators with existing arrangements for teacher preparation, in a context of teacher shortage in some subjects and areas: all underlined for teacher educators the need to maintain high standards in BEd and PGCE courses.

The new CATE came into official existence on 1 January 1990. The principal structural differences from earlier arrangements are a rather smaller Council, a larger secretariat, with two half-time professional officers and more administrative support; a more substantial and consistent role for local committees, which will undertake some of the work formerly undertaken by the Council's reporting groups; and terms of reference that include developmental functions and opportunities to offer advice to the Secretary of State on the operation of the criteria and on such other matters as he might propose.

The new criteria reflect the experience of the previous five years and the introduction of the National Curriculum in both primary and secondary education. They are in important respects more explicit than those they replace. For example, the '100 hours' requirement now includes science as well as mathematics and English; it is laid down that tutors should have a minimum of 35 days' school experience in each five years of service; the phasing of students' teaching practice is spelled out; there is more detail (particularly in the commentary that accompanies the criteria) about teacher involvement in planning and delivering courses, and in student selection and assessment; the subjects that primary-phase students should be prepared through curriculum courses to teach are stated, and some of the competencies that students should have acquired by the end of their course are specified.

Conclusion

Although this chapter has focused on the work of the Council for the Accreditation of Teacher Education, there are a number of other bodies that also exercise control over teacher education. The number of student-teacher places that will be funded in universities, polytechnics and colleges is determined by the Universities Funding Council and Polytechnics and Colleges Funding Council respectively, but in close collaboration with the Department of Education and Science. The academic validation of courses remains the responsibility of the CNAA in the Polytechnics and Colleges, and of individual chartered universities. Although there will be no early repetition of the comprehensive round of full inspections of initial-teacher-training institutions undertaken by HMI between 1983 and 1987, inspections and visits will continue to take place and be publicly reported upon.

The National Curriculum Council (NCC) and Schools Examination and Assessment Council both have interests in the way in which teachers are prepared and certificated, and the NCC has set up a professional development committee. An important function for the new CATE will be to ensure that all the different bodies that exert influence in this field remain in regular contact with one another, as well as with those in the field from whom valuable new ideas can come in the years ahead. There is no lack of work to be done if the best practice is to become more widely disseminated, and control exercised in a way that ensures the proper professional and public accountability of teacher-education institutions in an atmosphere in which innovation and new initiatives can flourish.

Chapter 8

The Control of Teacher Education: A General Teaching Council for England and Wales

Alec Ross

Introduction

This chapter is an account of repeated attempts by the teaching profession in England and Wales to create what is an essential part of a properly articulated professional structure – that is, a means whereby the profession itself controls entry to the profession, standards of discipline and procedures leading to dismissal from the profession. Such a body would at the same time provide a voice capable of speaking on behalf of the profession as a whole. The chapter, in other words, concerns the creation of a General Teaching Council for England and Wales. (These two countries are specified because the Scots, ever forward in matters which concern the quality of what is provided in that nation's schools, have had such a council since 1965.)

The word 'repeated' is used in the first sentence because this is an account of many failed attempts; the objective has still not been achieved. Despite these failures there continues to be widespread support in the teaching profession for such a council: it remains as the long-term objective of the teaching profession. Politicians inevitably have to think in the shorter term and the success story, if such it be, told elsewhere in this volume, is of politicians in a hurry using the full panoply of power, resources and influence available to them to take over territory left empty by a teaching profession more concerned with day-to-day tactics than with long-term strategies. The telling of the tale from the point of view of the profession itself may, however, help governments and teachers to see more clearly how best to create the means whereby the profession itself, whose members carry the major responsibility for the quality of what is offered in the nation's schools, is given its proper place in the regulation of that profession.

Historical perspective

Though this chapter concentrates on the last three decades it would be wrong not to take brief note of earlier attempts, going back to the middle of the nineteen century, to create a professional body for the teaching profession. The College of Preceptors, a body which deserves praise for its never-ceasing endeavours across the years to keep alive the idea of a professional body, received its Royal Charter in 1849. Following the creation of a General Medical Council in 1860 the College of Preceptors brought forward a proposal for a similar body for the teaching profession through a Scholastic Registration Act. Balchin (1981) begins his historical account of these developments by quoting *The Educational Times* of January 1862:

> A Scholastic Council formed on a plan analogous to the constitution of the General Medical Council would represent the interests of Education and of Educators, without favour or partiality towards any particular system of Education.

This early attempt was followed by several other abortive efforts on behalf of the growing profession. The establishment of a Teachers' Registration Council in 1902 was followed in 1929 by the Royal Society of Teachers which was finally abolished by Order in Council in 1949. In reviewing these various failed attempts, a Department of Education and Science Working Party which reported in 1970 (Department of Education and Science, 1970 and hereafter called, after its chairman, the Weaver Report), concluded that 'all the earlier attempts to set up a professional body for teachers had one weakness in common – that registration was not compulsory' (p 2). Here, and not for the first time, a point of principle emerges: mandatory registration, the essential element, can only be implemented by government fiat. There is, however, a measure of reluctance on the part of any government to introduce legislation which is itself dependent on the decisions of an outside body. The point is particularly apposite in relation to a profession almost entirely employed in a publicly provided service for which that government has direct responsibility. Two sides are needed to make a contract; if one side is unwilling no contract is made.

In recent times the movement towards a General Teaching Council reached one of its periodic peaks in the 1960s and achieved a notable success in Scotland in 1965. The Scottish development had its origins in a strike by Glasgow teachers on the twin (and not unrelated) issues of remuneration and dilution. By the latter was meant the introduction of untrained teachers into a system which had always placed high value on proper training for this most important of vocations. The unrest led to the setting up of a committee, under the chairmanship of Lord Wheatley,

> to review, in the light of the requirements of the education service and the practice in relation to other professions, the present arrangements for the award and withdrawal of certificates of competency to teach, and to make recommendations regarding any changes that are considered desirable in these arrangements and any consequential changes in the functions of teacher training authorities (quoted in Miller, 1981).

What is to be noted here is the exclusion of matters concerned with the pay and conditions of service of practising teachers and the emphasis on establishing the criteria for admission to the profession. The committee had a majority of certificated teachers and when it reported in 1963 its central recommendation was the creation of

> new machinery . . . for the teaching profession and that there should be established a General Teaching Council for Scotland broadly similar in scope, powers and functions to the Councils in other professions (Miller, 1981).

The cross-reference to the General Medical Council and similar bodies is also noteworthy. During the general-election campaign which followed in the autumn of 1964, William Ross, an ex-school teacher who was destined to become Secretary of State for Scotland, promised that if elected he would seek to create a General Teaching Council for Scotland. He and his party were elected and he forthwith introduced a bill which in due course became the Teaching Council (Scotland) Act, 1965. Miller (1981) provides a short account of the workings of the Council and a fuller statement will be found in the General Teaching Council for Scotland's *Handbook* (4th edition, 1981). The Council maintains a register of teachers qualified to teach in Scotland, keeps training courses under review and makes recommendations thereon to the Secretary of State; it also considers and makes recommendations to the Secretary of State on 'matters (other than remuneration and conditions of service) relating to the supply of teachers'. It also keeps itself informed about the nature of the instruction given in training institutions. Of its 49 members, 30 are teachers directly elected by the 80,000 teachers on the register. Only teachers on the register can be employed in local-authority and grant-aided schools. The Council has the power to remove teachers from the register.

The powers granted to the General Teaching Council for Scotland are not unduly great but, in contrast with the situation in England and Wales, they do, whilst recognizing the ultimate authority of the Secretary of State for Scotland, give the teaching profession a recognized place in the organization and management of the profession. Instead of being left to provide observations on policy initiatives emanating from government, the Scottish teachers are able through the Council to initiate policy discussions. Thomasson (1969) points out that the one recommendation of the Wheatley Committee which the government did not act upon was the proposal that where the Secretary of State wished to proceed in a manner not approved by the Council, he should be required to state and defend his policy in both Houses of Parliament. Neither the government, nor indeed the opposition, could accept this since it would have made parliamentary procedure subject to the approval of an outside body. There is a real constitutional issue here but the Scottish experience provides a satisfactory answer: in the event of a difference arising, the government publishes its proposals and teachers, like any other members of the public, are at liberty to campaign against them with a view to influencing parliament. This constitutional point is certainly no reason for resisting the creation of a professional body, though it has from time to time been used by those anxious to prevent the emergence of a professional body for the teaching profession.

The 1964 general election which brought William Ross to the post of Secretary of State for Scotland led, south of the border, to a succession of Labour Secretaries of State for Education and Science. Michael Stewart (1964–5) was followed by Anthony Crosland (1965–7) who was less concerned with teachers than with comprehensive schools and the new polytechnics. Patrick Gordon-Walker's stay (1967–8) was brief.

A final attempt at setting up a GTC for England and Wales, the Weaver Report

The Scottish advance had been noted south of the border and in 1966 a committee representing all the teachers' unions and associations in England and Wales urged the Secretary of State to set up an official working party to prepare a plan for the creation of a General Teaching Council for England and Wales. The reply was most discouraging: the proposal 'would involve a transfer of control over the fundamental matter of teachers' recruitment from the Government to the proposed Council' (quoted in Balchin, 1981). Evidently it was feared that a union-dominated professional body might conceivably raise entry standards to the point at which a shortage of recruits would be created.

It should be recalled that this correspondence took place at a time when teacher training was undergoing one of its regular fundamental changes: the B Ed, a four-year initial-training programme, had begun to produce its first graduates and the level of entry qualifications possessed by entrants to the training institutions was rising fast. There was much talk in the profession about making teaching a graduate-entry profession. There was repeated pressure for the DES to establish an enquiry into the teaching profession, but as Fred Willey, the member of parliament who was later to chair a Select Committee of the Commons which did carry out an enquiry into teacher education in the session 1969–70, put it, the DES had for years 'resisted repeated calls from responsible bodies for an investigation into teacher training' (Willey and Maddison, 1971, p 8).

There is further evidence of DES resistance to outside policy groups. Under the 1944 Education Act there was a statutory requirement to maintain an outside advisory group, the Central Advisory Council. Over the years this body had produced a series of major reports which had a considerable impact upon the development of education. When what turned out to be the last of these reports was published in 1967 there was clearly an in-house decision not to reappoint the Council even though this was a statutory requirement. The Commons Select Committee in the session 1969–70 was able to extract from the embarrassed officials the admission that despite the legal requirement nothing had been done to keep the Council in being (see evidence at Q 1244ff on 21st April 1970; Minutes of Evidence of the Select Committee of Education and Science 1969–70). The Council never met again and the matter was not regularized until 1986 when the legal requirement was removed. Given this context it was not therefore surprising that the teacher representatives received such a cool reception. Obviously, outside bodies can cause undue difficulties for governments and their civil servants; such bodies could be said to have power (to make recommendations, for example) without responsibility (for example to find the resources needed to implement those recommendations). Such a view moves one towards a reluctance to have groups which cannot be controlled; if an outside group cannot be avoided it had better be small and capable of being 'managed'. It would also be better if the group consisted not of representatives (as the unions were proposing) but of nominated individuals appointed in a personal capacity.

Whatever may have been the in-house policy amongst the officials, civil servants are subject to the wishes of their political masters. A cabinet reshuffle in the spring of 1968 brought to the DES an ex-teacher, Edward Short, later to be Lord Glenamara. By mid-August of the same year he had issued a circular letter to all local education authorities advising them of the importance he attached to including teachers among the persons of experience in education who must, under the terms of the Education Act of 1944, be included in every education committee (Department of Education and Science, 1968a). On the 4th of October, speaking to the Newcastle Teachers' Association, he held out the prospect of self-government for teachers. 'Self-government for the profession,' he said, has long been among the declared objectives of the National Union of Teachers, and I hope that I may be able to bring it a considerable step nearer. The government must continue to have a close interest in teacher supply, and therefore in matters affecting entry to the profession. But self-government is a mark of professional maturity and I am hopeful that a system can be devised that will be broadly acceptable to all concerned (Department of Education and Science, 1968b).

By the following spring (April 1969) and after informal discussions with the teacher associations, the DES had produced a memorandum entitled 'A possible framework for a Teaching Council for England and Wales'. The Secretary of State followed this up by setting up in July 1969 a working party to examine, using the memorandum as a guide,

proposals for the establishment and operation of a council through which teachers in England and Wales can exercise a measure of professional self-government; and for national arrangements by which advice can be made available to the Secretary of State on matters relating to the training and supply of teachers (Department of Education and Science, 1970, p 1).

The teacher associations were strongly represented on the working party and it was chaired by a senior DES official, T R (later Sir Toby) Weaver. It is noteworthy that Short's 'self-government' is prominent in the terms of reference, but the passage following the semi-colon is also of significance since it gave expression to concern within the DES that any future arrangements should leave with the Secretary of State that measure of control needed to ensure that he was able to carry out the duties in relation to teacher supply assigned to him in the 1944 Act.

The working party reported early in 1970 in a report proudly entitled *A Teaching Council for England and Wales* (Department of Education and Science, 1970) and it is commonly known by the name of its chairman as the Weaver Report. It offers a sensible set of thoroughly worked out practical proposals, even including a chapter on how a teaching council could be financed. With regard to the two distinguishable issues of self-government and teacher supply, it recommended that there be two separate bodies, one for each of the issues. The 'self-government' body would have a majority of teachers while the 'supply' committee would not. The first body would be the Teaching Council and the second an Advisory Council on the Supply and Training of Teachers (ACSTT). The Council would not have its members directly elected as in Scotland but appointed by the teacher associations. Only five of the 29 members of the supply committee would be teachers.

Developments after the Weaver Report

The report was widely discussed in the teaching profession but was rejected by the National Union of Teachers at its annual conference in 1971. Immediately prior to that conference the union's periodical *The Teacher* (March 1971) produced a somewhat tendentious account of the proposals. It began by referring to two recent cases of doctors appearing before the General Medical Council on charges of professional misconduct: 'Some doctors think the Council Victorian and superfluous', it claimed, and went on to ask 'Would a teaching council satisfy teachers?' The executive committee of the NUT had given more serious consideration to the report before recommending its rejection in its present form. It wanted teachers to have two-thirds of the seats on the Council and the supply committee to be a sub-committee of the Council and have a majority of teachers. The NUT also wanted the Council to cover private as well as maintained schools. On the question of how to deal with conflicts between the Secretary of State and the Council the NUT called for the affirmative resolution procedure (ie arguing the case in parliament) instead of the recommended procedure of laying an order on the table of the House of Commons.

What we can see emerging from this decision of the NUT is a further point which supporters of the General Teaching Council have to take into account. For the lack of a professional body capable of representing teachers as a whole, the professional associations have themselves been compelled to extend their role to deal with matters which in other circumstances would have been dealt with by a professional body. A General Teaching Council has, therefore, not only to claw back powers from government (such as dismissal from the profession) which should never have gone there but also to persuade professional associations to recognize the existence of a body charged with speaking authoritatively on a range of professional matters. The current unwillingness of government to take teachers into their confidence is in part due to the fact that without a Teaching Council the only bodies to deal with are unions; a decision not to discuss such issues with unions has thus led to teachers as a whole being deprived of the opportunity to have their views represented. Another result of unions taking on responsibility for the whole range of professional matters has, of course, been that with the profession divided between several unions it has been all too easy to divide and rule.

The NUT decision of 1971 was, therefore, significant but it is a matter of conjecture whether a favourable decision would have led to the formation of a General Teaching Council, for in the summer of 1970 the government fell and interest shifted to a more general enquiry into teacher education. Though the DES had resisted such an enquiry the Conservative Shadow Secretary of State, Margaret Thatcher, had at the hustings promised such an enquiry. Once elected, the new Secretary of State, always a woman of her word, implemented her promise and set up a short, sharp 'inquiry' into teacher education and training carried out by a small and carefully selected group of experts under the chairmanship of Lord James of Rusholme. This was in marked contrast to the constitution of the Weaver working party which, being representative, was necessarily large. The representative committees of the 1960s had to be large because, there being no Teaching Council, the only way to get the teaching profession represented was to invite all the many unions to send representatives and to face up to sterile arguments about how many representatives each body could have. Such large committees came, not entirely unjustly, to be disparaged as a 'stage army' of mandated representatives required to 'report back' before agreeing to anything. The preface to the Weaver Report (Department of Education and Science, 1970, p iv) makes it clear that the members were unable to commit their parent bodies. The argument for a small, tight committee of nominated members could, therefore, in the light of experience over the previous decade, be strongly made.

Lord James's committee certainly worked quickly and its report *Teacher Education and Training* (Department of Education and Science, 1972) appeared in January 1972. The only reference to the Weaver proposals is a footnote indicating that the term 'registered teacher' (a term used in the report) 'is not intended to prejudge the outcome of current discussions of the possible establishment of a Teaching Council'. The shift away from large representative committees could well have had an influence upon the fact that the major issue of a Teaching Council was not dealt with in this important report. The smaller committee of nominated people appointed 'in a personal capacity' is, of course, the model for the current Council for the Accreditation of Teacher Education (CATE).

The Weaver Report of 1970, following on from the Scottish Teaching Council (Registration) Act of 1965, could be regarded as the high point of the campaign for a General Teaching Council for England and Wales. With hindsight it can now be seen as an opportunity missed. From the point of view of those within the DES who were opposed to the idea it could no doubt be regarded as having been a near-run thing. The familiar world of the 1960s was beginning to change and the advent of the new government was only one marker of that change. The professions, and most notably those engaged in publicly provided services faced what was to be a turbulent decade. The Weaver-Report model was an expression of 1960s thinking; while the case for a General Teaching Council remains as strong as it ever was a prescription for the 1990s in no way mirrors what the government was prepared to offer in the early part of 1970.

As soon as the new administration took over it was advised that because of the continuing decline in the birth rate (it had peaked as long before as 1964) it was necessary to reduce the number of people entering the profession. In due course the Advisory Council on the Supply and Training of Teachers (ACSTT) – that is the 'supply' committee of the Weaver Report – was brought into being to help tackle the problem. Only the DES itself had the data needed and the committee was serviced and managed by the DES with assistance from Her Majesty's Inspectorate (HMI). ACSTT, being a representative committee, was able to play an important part in persuading the profession (and not least the teacher-training part of it which was most directly affected) that the quite radical measures taken were justifiable.

Meanwhile, throughout the 1970s the teacher associations regularly rehearsed the arguments for a Teaching Council; motions in support of such a council regularly appeared on the agenda of annual meetings. The arrival of a Labour government in 1974 led some to believe that the time had come to retrieve the errors of 1970 but it was always difficult to get agreement between the different associations as to how best to approach the problem. The most determined attempt took place in November 1978 with a meeting between the two largest unions, the National Union of Teachers (NUT) and the National Association of Schoolmasters and Union of Women Teachers (NAS/UWT). Agreement could not be reached since the NUT would not accept the Weaver Report of 1970 as the basis of the discussions but wanted a council with the much stronger teacher representation it had called for in 1971. Terry Casey, the General Secretary of the NAS/UWT had obviously become aware of significant shifts in public attitudes towards professions and thought the 1970 proposal was well worth taking because it was unlikely to be bettered. 'Parliament,' he said, 'would never set up the sovereign teaching council the NUT wanted' (*Education* 3 November 1978). He went on to warn against seeking what he called 'monopoly control' of a teaching council.

An entirely new element had entered the debate: something which later became known as 'consumerism' and was applied in particular to the work of professions employed in the provision of a publicly provided service. The word itself brought in concepts derived from the market; in the same vein of thought some professions could be characterized as having established a 'producers' monopoly'. Professional bodies controlling their own entry standards could be regarded as acting in restraint of trade. Though this set of ideas was new to the debate about the General Teaching Council it was not new in the general debate about the place of the professions in modern societies. As early as 1966,

Timothy Raison (who was later to become a distinguished chairman of the Commons Select Committee in the 1980s) had written an article in *New Society* (18 August 1966) asking if the whole professional notion was itself obsolete. He quoted an Institute of Economic Affairs monograph by D S Lees, *Economic Consequences of the Professions* which declared that 'producers are there to serve the interests of consumers . . . their profits and other forms of income, including status, derive their *raison d'être* from the welfare of consumers.' Raison had a suggestion to make to the teachers: he noted how in the medical profession there was a distinction between the negotiating body (the British Medical Association) and the professional body (the General Medical Council) and wondered whether there might not be a similar professional body for teachers separate from the teacher unions (Raison, 1966). These attitudes towards the professions, and especially towards those employed in the services provided by government and local authorities grew in strength and became part of common thinking in the 1980s. Such changes in attitudes undoubtedly call for adjustments in the professions themselves; in the case in point, the NUT showed itself unable to make that adjustment in the 1970s; in the 1980s the NAS/UWT showed itself to be equally inflexible.

Disarray amongst the teacher unions made it all the more justifiable for the government quietly to move into areas which might properly be thought of as in the province of a professional body. Statutes (such as the 1944 Education Act) are written in broad terms (especially in giving supervisory duties to the minister) and they have to be interpreted. General supervisory powers can be interpreted as justifying intervention on points of detail even when those matters have by custom and practice been left to others. In relation to teachers, the ACSTT – and even more its successor body of 1980, the Advisory Council on the Supply and Education of Teachers (ACSET) – proved to be extremely useful to the DES in introducing a number of measures designed to bring the profession and especially its training arm under central control. The change in title of the advisory body was regarded by some as indicating the de facto extension into matters which went well beyond straightforward questions of supply. In due course the representative ACSET was allowed to lapse and the present small, nominated body, CATE, was set up in 1984 and placed on a permanent basis in 1989. Thus what had started out as a representative 'supply' committee designed to be part of a General Teaching Council had gradually been transformed into a nominated committee which did not deal with 'supply' at all but concentrated upon the most important task of any professional council – determining entry to that profession. Supply matters were quietly taken back into the DES where they remain. The profession as a profession has now been eliminated from all formal consultations affecting both professional standards and the supply of teachers.

The key which opened the door to these significant developments was a circular issued in 1978 (9/78) which declared that all entrants to teacher-training courses must possess certain minimum standards in mathematics and English language. There could be no possible objection to these requirements but they are to be noted because of what, by incremental accretion, was built on them. In so far as there was a debate on Circular 9/78 it was overtaken by the bigger national debate which led to the fall of the Labour government in 1979 and the arrival in Downing Street as prime minister of Margaret Thatcher, who was to hold that office right through the 1980s and continues to do so as the next decade unfolds. The first Secretary of State in the new administration (Mark Carlisle 1979–81) busied himself with tidying up the uncertain situation left in the aftermath of the 'Great Debate on Education', as it was called, generated in 1976 by the previous prime minister, James (later Lord) Callaghan. Carlisle's successor, Sir Keith (later Lord) Joseph held the office for a remarkably long period (1981–6).

Soon after taking office Sir Keith Joseph turned his attention to teachers, their training and the standards of their work in the classrooms. *Teaching Quality* (Department of Educational Science, 1983b) which he issued in 1983, laid down the framework of what was in due course to be the system of centralized political control introduced by Circular 3/84 (Welsh Office, 21/84). This system is described and analysed elsewhere in this volume (see chapter 7). Here it has to be said that as a substitute for a professional body it suffers from grave deficiencies. However apolitical the members (all nominated by the Secretary of State) of CATE may be it remains a political body required to go 'with the grain' of public policy as laid down by the government of the day. The criteria it uses in judging the acceptability of courses permitting those who are successful to enter the teaching profession, are handed down to them by the Secretary of State. The organization itself is physically located in the offices of the DES and is serviced by DES officials. The local committees upon which CATE relies for part of its work are subject to its approval. The first change of government involving a change of political party will expose the unstable nature of this substitute for a professional accrediting body of the kind other professions have. Such a change of government would inevitably lead to an entire revision of the criteria in order to give expression to the new philosophy and priorities and perhaps to eliminate some of the old ones, the members of the Council itself would, no doubt, be replaced by a new set of nominees and the inspectors who scrutinize courses on behalf of CATE would have to be provided with new criteria. All courses would have to be rewritten and re-accredited.

The elimination of the profession from policy making: the consequences

The elimination of the profession, as a profession, from discussions about the gradual adjustment of professional courses to the changing needs of the service, deprives the organization of the accumulated experience of the profession itself. Furthermore, politically necessitated sudden changes of the kind instanced above, quite apart from demeaning the profession, lead to discontinuity in the development of the profession and its training. There is also the danger that decisions taken centrally and imposed on the whole system may be mistaken. In top-down systems designed to operate without a countervailing bottom-up corrective element, a fever at the top rapidly infects the whole system. It is surprising that a government strongly dedicated to freedom, enterprise, innovation and entrepreneurship should, in matters of education, have imposed a command structure which deprives the professional people concerned of opportunities to use the very qualities which the system is meant to foster.

One of the glories of our educational system has been the freedom it provided for innovation and experiment. Indeed many much-criticized experiments of the past were in time adopted by the system as a whole and became part of a new orthodoxy. The classic role of HMI was to appraise the wide range and variety of practice they were privileged to witness and to distil from this ever-growing body of experience the principles of what they judged at that time to be good practice. Thus, both directly and indirectly, practitioners were able to make their contribution to the development of practice. Today, and especially in the field of teacher training, individual courses have to be checked against a list of requirements supplied by the Secretary of State. This is, of course, an endemic flaw in highly centralized command-structure systems and it is necessary to add that there is more than one form of authoritarianism: there are professional bodies in other fields which, in their accreditation procedures, are subject to all the criticisms which can be made of the present system in teacher education in England and Wales.

Centralization is undoubtedly administratively the tidiest, and functionally — at any rate in the short term — the most efficient system whereby a department of state can control the activity for which it has responsibility. This may not, however, be the case in relation to a service which, unlike industry from which the command structure approach was drawn, involves a high involvement of professionals at the point at which the service is delivered to the public. Short-term advantages do not predicate long-term success. Crude 'manage-the-workforce' techniques unthinkingly taken over from business practice as developed in the middle management of industry are not necessarily apposite to the professional work involved in education. They could even be counterproductive. Furthermore, the infinite number of variations in professional behaviour which necessarily have to be developed in order to provide such an individualized service as education, is such that even an army of clipboard-bearing inspectors could not adequately monitor how far the centrally determined criteria were being met at any one time. In short, a service which involves intensive use of professional people at the point of delivery has firstly to trust those professionals and secondly must build into its management means whereby the collective views of those same professionals can be used to shape the future provision of that service.

The traditional way in which professions exercise control over their members is that of peer scrutiny, which is particularly effective when the professional body itself determines who shall have the licence to practise. Such procedures may not be directly applicable to the activities of something approaching half a million teachers going about their daily classroom work but that is no proper reason for failing to recognize that the profession itself, as a profession, has the right to be consulted about the professional matters which have to be taken into account when planning the service. In particular, where matters of quality of provision are concerned, it shows a misunderstanding of the nature of the task not to include the teaching profession itself in the management of the profession. Put bluntly, the teaching profession is not a workforce to be managed, a group of unruly operatives to be disciplined nor a union to be tamed; it is what it says it is, a profession dedicated to teaching and it deserves the respect due to men and women who to a large extent, given their training and qualifications, could earn higher salaries in other occupations but who remain in teaching because that is their vocation. It is this group of professionals, and only this group, which can provide that full range of rewarding experiences which are needed if the nation's children are to develop and to fulfil themselves in such a way as to bring credit to themselves, their families and their country. To exclude such people from the higher counsels of the service is not only ill-advised; it is potentially damaging to the future prosperity of the nation.

Sir Keith Joseph retired to the House of Lords in 1986 and was succeeded by Kenneth Baker who, in three hectic years (1986–9), drove home the policies implicit in the Joseph legacy. The current Secretary of State, John MacGregor, faces a growing crisis in teacher supply and the prospect of having to respond, later in 1990, to a Commons Select Committee which, judging by the all-but-unanimous evidence given to it, may well be asking why the DES has cold-shouldered all efforts to create a Teaching Council to help them manage a service which is in increasing difficulty on the matter of supply of teachers. The *Times Educational Supplement* of 2 June 1989 quoted a Gallup Poll showing that 80 per cent of teachers surveyed favoured a General Teaching Council to control professional standards: 'a topic', it went on to remark, 'about which the DES is doggedly evasive, because the only kind of GTC worth having would have to have teeth and a life of its own and this would never do.'

Relationships between the government and the teaching profession have, during the course of the 1980s, been entirely altered for a number of reasons including union mishandling of professional matters and government determination to take into its own hands control of the teaching profession. Even if we were to leave to one side the Teachers' Pay and Conditions Act 1987, which removed from the profession its negotiating rights in matters concerned with remuneration, it is still true to say that the teaching profession in England and Wales is now under the direct control of central government and its nominated bodies. At no place in the system is there provision for formal consultation with the profession *as a profession* on professional matters. This was brought fully home in 1989 when, as part of a larger package which contained several sensible things, the DES introduced an entirely new category of 'licensed' teachers who could be recruited with only two years of post-A-level education, employed as teachers and trained on the job by their employers. It is hardly surprising that a profession which had struggled for so long to become one to which entry was obtained by successfully completing a degree and a training course did not welcome that proposal. It remains to be seen whether this new scheme will be used in any significant way. As far as is known, this proposal was not considered by the government's own body, CATE.

New thinking on a General Teaching Council

This attack has to be seen in the context of an assault, already referred to, on the professions generally, and especially upon those engaged in the provision of publicly managed services. Neither law nor medicine escaped and it is evident that if either of these professions were today to seek the charters they obtained when they were first established the terms available to them would to be much more restricted. Teachers do not have the protection of custom and practice built up over a long period and their future plans must therefore recognize the changed circumstances. A newly created Teaching Council would provide a splendid opportunity to draw up the kind of charter appropriate to a profession practising in the twenty-first century.

It was inevitable that the developments outlined above should have produced a reaction from the teacher associations. An initiative came in an uplanned way at the annual meeting at the end of 1983 of the Universities Council for the Education of Teachers (UCET); a body which represents university interests in teacher education. Delegates from teacher associations present at the meeting, including those from the independent sector, pressed UCET to provide what might be called neutral ground upon which discussions between the unions and other interested associations could take place with a view, yet again, to trying to create a General Teaching Council. UCET agreed and a series of meetings under its auspices began; they continue to this day. The meetings are chaired by the present writer and the technical working party is chaired by John Sayer, head of the University of London Institute of Education's Education Management Unit. A draft constitution has been published (Education Management Unit, 1989) which deals with all standard issues such as role and function, registration, financing and relationship with other bodies and there is a suggested constitution of the governing Council which includes a majority of teachers. With regard to 'supply' matters the proposed Council would advise, but on questions of admission to and dismissal from the profession the Council would determine.

The meetings have not been without their internal tensions since it has to be remembered that the mid-1980s was a period of considerable disruption in the schools. Nevertheless, it noteworthy that a group of 17 teacher and other interested associations, covering between them both the independent and the maintained sectors of education, have continued in existence and have provided a focus for the growing number of teachers and others pressing the government to consider again the question of creating a General Teaching Council. Though the DES has on an informal basis been kept informed, it is obvious that if real discussions are to start there must, on behalf of the group, be a formal approach to the government. Unfortunately the Teachers' Pay and Conditions Act of 1987 had such a damaging impact upon relationships between government and the profession that the NAS/UWT declared that it had lost all confidence in the even-handedness of the Secretary of State in matters concerned with the control of the profession and that it was therefore unwilling to support any formal approach being made to the government. In particular it expressed its fear that the government might use the opportunity to create a Teaching Council which would be an arm of government rather than a body representative of professional judgements.

The fullest direct response from the Secretary of State is in a letter to the writer dated 29 November 1988:

My position on the idea of a General Teaching Council has not changed. I have, however, always said that I would be happy to consider a proposal from others for a General Teaching Council that commanded widespread support from, and was likely to serve the interests of, *all* relevant parties; including parents and employers as well as teachers. In the absence of such a proposal, however, I do not intend to take any initiative to change the present arrangements for the regulation of the profession, which in general work well and to the benefit of all concerned.

Mr Baker no doubt considered that having set such an impossible criterion before the matter could even be discussed it would not reappear on his desk. Nevertheless, the group began a series of discussions with a wider range of bodies including employers' and parents' organizations. When this was reported to Mr Baker his reply was brief but perfectly clear. A letter to the author dated 19 January 1989 states:

I do not intend at present to initiate any action to establish a General Teaching Council. I should however be happy to receive a further report from you once you have completed your consultations with employers, parents and other groups.

The government had to give a fuller explanation of its position a few months later when Lord Glenamara (who appears earlier in this narrative as Edward Short, Secretary of State for Education and Science from 1968 to 1970) brought before the House of Lords a motion asking the government whether it would establish a General Teaching Council (Hansard, 5 April 1989). Rarely can the case have been more expertly and movingly put; the difficulties which had befallen earlier attempts were noted and the necessity for government to reserve some powers was fully acknowledged but the case overall was so convincing that the only speaker to offer opposition to the motion was the government spokesman. 'I am not advocating a General Teaching Council simply as a means of enabling the government to make amends to the teachers for all the indignities they have suffered in recent years,' Lord Glenamara said,

but because it is surely a sensible, democratic and efficient course to take at this time, if the government want a teaching service of high quality with pride in itself, to carry out the 1988 reforms. It is worth remembering that only the teachers can make a success of the 1988 Education Reform Act – only the teachers, not the DES nor anybody else.

He took it as axiomatic that a General Teaching Council should control 'the entry to and egress from their profession' and said that from this a number of other functions would flow. 'Clearly teachers must have a major voice in the training of teachers, both the initial training and the in-service training, *but* as the Inns of Court . . . and the Law Society have a major voice in the training of lawyers.' A General Teaching Council was not, he said, an end in itself 'but it could be a means of achieving a high degree of unity of purpose in carrying out the public will, as expressed in legislation passed by parliament on education, in the best possible way. It could help to create a recognized, respected profession united in public service.'

Lord Beloff declared that

> it is wrong to think that the existence of autonomous professions in any sense detracts from the national interest. Properly viewed, self-governing, autonomous professions contribute to the national interest by enabling people to express their own devotion to the particular tasks which they have to perform. If that is generally true, it must be true of teachers.

He thought that public confidence in the teaching profession 'would be greater if teachers' corporate contribution was made largely through a General Teaching Council, and the unions were left to what is their natural habitat: negotiations on matters of pay, hours of work, length of holidays and so forth.' Lord Taylor of Blackburn and Lord McNair agreed that a General Teaching Council would help to restore morale whilst Lord Dormand of Easington called for the government itself to take the initiative. Baroness David reminded members that Scotland provided a model 'that is known to work'. Replying on behalf of the government Lord Henley said that ministers took every opportunity to praise teachers but that he could not give a yes-or-no answer to Lord Glenamara's question: will the government establish a General Teaching Council for England and Wales? He referred to the 1970 initiative; there had, he said, been a failure to find unanimity of purpose across the profession. 'A General Teaching Council is not an idea whose time has come,' he said, and creating such a council was not a priority for the government. 'We have no present intention of establishing one or of taking any initiative to change the present arrangements for the regulation of the profession. Lord Henley thought that teachers were different from doctors and lawyers, who are largely self-employed. He wanted evidence that there is a demand from teachers for such a council and that such a body would serve the interests of all parties concerned and not just the teachers. He ended with an expression of hope that the House would agree 'that the government have been and continue to be open and fair-minded on this important question.'

Mr Baker's successor, John MacGregor, took office on 26 July 1989 and his initial position has been one of 'agnosticism'. Nevertheless he agreed in June 1990 to see members of the UCET Forum to hear the arguments in favour of a General Teaching Council. This, no doubt, was part of his preparation for a response to the Report of the Select committee of the House of Commons on Education, Science and Arts, which, in its second report, issued in April 1990 (208–1), recommended (p ix) 'that the Government create a General Teaching Council to work for the enhancement of the profession.'

The initiative for which UCET provides the forum was frequently referred to in the Lords debate; it has never, however, been able to enter into direct discussions with government, for reasons explained above. Clearly progress cannot be made if the government of the day is unwilling because some of the key powers (admission to the profession, for example, and dismissal therefrom) are at present lodged with the Secretary of State who is clearly anxious to continue to use those powers without having to discuss their use with any outside body. Her Majesty's Opposition have been rather more encouraging. A policy document (Labour Party, 1989) written by the Labour Party education team led by Jack Straw, Shadow Secretary of State, offers a realistic appraisal of the present and likely future situation. What the authors call a 'proper professional structure' would provide 'a focus for cohesion' and a means whereby the peer group could establish and enforce standards. Such a body could also give advice to government on supply and training questions. 'But,' it continues, 'the age of the autonomous professional is now over. All professions now have to accept a much higher degree of external accountability for their actions than hitherto.' The paper argues that this shift towards more accountability strengthens the case for what it calls ' a proper professional structure'.

> We shall therefore carefully consider the establishment of a General Teachers' [sic] Council . . . we are strongly of the opinion that if it is to gain credibility with the public as well as the profession its members should be directly elected . . . rather than nominated. There would also have to be representation of the academic institutions and strong lay representation.

The triumph of the highly centralized, top–down, politically directed, command-structure approach to the problem of regulating the teaching profession can be explained on the one hand in terms of officials anxious to get a grip on an expensive system over which, despite their ultimate responsibility, they had insufficient control; and on the other, of politicians who, having learned from their civil servants how, despite custom and practice, existing latent powers could be recovered, decided to do that very thing in order to accomplish their political objectives. It might even be hypothesized that the revolution begun by the civil servants was hijacked by the politicians. All that is, however, only one part of the explanation; the other part of it has to do with a woefully divided profession concerned more with short-term aims, sometimes related to inter-union rivalries, than with long-term strategies for enhancing the position of the profession as a whole. Teaching needs its unions but it also needs an overarching professional body to carry out the functions which no union, nor indeed alliance of unions, can satisfactorily fulfil.

However, the Labour Party is right to point out that a Teaching Council created today would of necessity not be constituted on the lines of the classic professional bodies created in the mid-nineteenth century. It would also be constructed on different lines from those laid down by the Weaver Report (Department of Education and Science, 1970). It must, of course, stay out of discussions about pay and conditions; that is the responsibility of the teacher unions and whatever body represents the employers. It must, however, in keeping with the spirit of the times, avoid being a 'providers' monopoly'; the best way to achieve that is to ensure that the consumers – employers, parents and the general public – are well represented. There must obviously be an important place for the government of the day; reserved powers to protect the constitutional position of the Secretary of State would be essential. It would also be necessary clearly to distinguish between those matters which the Council could determine and those upon which it could advise. Other professional bodies could provide valuable advice and some of the government nominations might properly be used to ensure that important interests (the churches come to mind), otherwise unrepresented, would be able to make their contribution.

The only Council capable of carrying out its functions would be one covering the independent as well as the maintained sectors so that it would be clear that only those registered with the Council could be employed as teachers. For at least a decade the scope of the Council should be limited to those teachers working with children and students of statutory school age. Only then might it be possible to begin considering whether to bring all who bear the title 'teacher' into the organization. For all this to be brought about it would be necessary for the teachers' unions to re-appraise the question of how best to have professional views represented to government. At the same time it would be necessary for a wise government to consider carefully the arguments put by Lord Glenamara in the debate in the House of Lords in April 1989; such a government would welcome, not resist, the creation of a body through which the profession, as a profession, could be consulted. Of course, educational questions have, in recent years, become political questions as the post-war consensus broke down; but these are short-term considerations. In the long run political questions are educational questions in the sense that the values we all wish to see developed and enhanced in a democratic society should themselves be demonstrated in the functioning of the very system charged with the task of nurturing those same values in the minds and attitudes of the next generation.

Conclusion

No profession today is, or should seek to be, wholly autonomous; in teaching, as in other professions closely involved in a publicly provided service, the place of government must be fully acknowledged. Governments, however, should consider the value, when dealing with professions upon whose skill and commitment the quality of the service provided depends, of a self-denying ordinance. For civil servants who are not themselves members of that profession to seek to prescribe in detail how that profession should be organized and how it should conduct its professional work can only be, in the long term, counterproductive. Quality is determined not by a vote in the Houses of Parliament or by a circular from the DES but by the actions of professionals in their day-to-day work with their clients. Lord Wheatley's report of 1963, which led in due course to the Teaching Council (Scotland) Act of 1965, pointed out that qualified teachers 'constitute the largest single group of well-qualified, highly educated people in the country'; he went on to point out, however, that it was a profession in which 'there is a widespread dissatisfaction on certain matters . . . due at least in part, to the feeling that the profession is consistently undervalued'. *The Times* in a leader commenting on Lord Wheatley's report (27 June 1963) thought it 'historically appropriate that proposals for an upward valuation of the teaching profession should originate in that country' and went on to suggest that the report should also be studied in England and Wales 'where similar feelings of professional inferiority are not uncommon'. The fact that three decades later England and Wales are still without a professional body to represent this most important of professions is nothing less than shameful.

Chapter 9

The Future of Teacher Education

Denis Lawton

The title of this chapter seems to be an invitation to speculate. It would be possible to map out existing trends and to project those trends ten years or so into the future. But that would be to assume (or speculate) that the existing trends will continue, and that no major new developments will take place. Bold assumptions! Morever, one of the more interesting features of teacher education in the 1980s was the emergence of contradictions. For example, the growing central control of teacher education by the Department of Education and Science (DES), on the one hand, and the desire for much greater, even complete, freedom of access into the profession on the other. It is difficult to envisage such contradictions continuing indefinitely. The plan of this chapter will be, first, to analyse some of the important trends affecting initial teacher education — *political, educational* and *demographic*; second, to speculate about the outcome of the tensions and contradictions within the system; and, finally, to speculate about the pressures which may be so great during the 1990s that dramatic changes will be required, rather than tinkering with, or trying to prop up, the existing obsolescent structure.

Political trends

Reference has already been made to the contradictory pressures from the centralist, dirigiste policies of the DES, and the right-wing decontrollers and deprofessionalizers. I have elsewhere (Lawton, 1984) described the growth in central control within education generally and, since the early 1980s, in teacher education. The most obvious manifestation was the invention and development of the Council for the Accreditation of Teacher Education (CATE) which Sir William Taylor has described in an earlier chapter.

It would be inappropriate to attempt to evaluate the work of CATE

here, but it is clear that CATE has established national standards for initial teacher education, and hence, indirectly, standards for entry into the profession. Although some of these 'criteria' were more controversial than others, most educationists would accept the desirability of having some national guidelines for courses which carry qualified-teacher status, and most would accept the desirability of raising standards for entry into the teaching profession. The strange irony is, however, that at precisely the same time as CATE was establishing new standards there were pressures from the political right to abandon all such controls and restrictions, even to abandon teacher training altogether (Hillgate Group, 1989; O'Hear, 1988; Cox, 1989). The compromise achieved during the late 1980s was to retain teacher training, with higher standards, but at the same time to introduce new routes into the profession, such as licensed teachers and articled teachers, with lower standards. For these new routes the emphasis is placed on training within the school rather than in institutions of higher education.
I suggest that this kind of compromise cannot continue indefinitely, and that some kind of rationalization of 'qualified-teacher status' will be essential to avoid the collapse of the traditional routes into teaching.

The contradiction/compromise cannot last for long because a kind of 'Gresham's Law' will begin to operate whereby poorly qualified teachers will drive out (or inhibit the recruitment of) well-qualified teachers. Why should a good graduate join a poorly paid profession where his graduate status and professional training appear to count for little or nothing? Apart from questions of equity, there will be a real danger that teaching will sink even further in public esteem and become less attractive as a career for men and women of ability. CATE may be able to do something to ensure that non-graduate unqualified 'licensed teachers' are required to reach some minimum standards, but that is unlikely to be enough to solve the problem.

In *The Tightening Grip* (1984) I suggested that it was a mistake to talk of 'DES views' or 'DES policies', since the DES was made up of at least three different groups each with its own preferences:

- *The politicos* (Conservative politicians and their political advisers) whose beliefs and values include 'the market' in education and freedom of choice.
- *The bureaucrats* (DES civil servants) who value good administration and efficiency above other matters.
- *The professionals* (HER Majesty's Inspectorate) who would give priority to encouraging professional standards and quality.

I suggested (p 17) that within this DES 'tension system' the three groups would have different wishes or priorities for a variety of policy issues: on curriculum, for example, the politicos are likely to be concerned about 'standards' and parental choice, the civil servants would like to clear lists of objectives, whereas Her Majesty's Inspectorate (HMI) developed a common curriculum model based on areas of experience. (In this case, the political and bureaucratic preferences prevailed over the professional and gave rise to the National Curriculum in 1987–8.)

Since then I have complicated the model further (Lawton, 1989) by suggesting that conservative politicians at the time leading up to the Education Reform Act (ERA) 1988 were themselves divided into two main groups – the privatizers and the minimalists – and that the ERA was itself a compromise. It is a mistake to look for a coherent policy on education in the ERA; what we find is a series of compromises, trying to resolve the differences between those who favour laissez-faire in education and those who want a state system of a minimal kind which gives good value for money and a supply of better-trained workers.

Applying this model specifically to teacher education we might arrive at the following:

- *The politicos* would like to improve the supply of teachers at the lowest possible cost (whilst preserving distinctions between independent and state education).
- *The bureaucrats* would prefer clear-cut criteria for entrants to the profession and for qualified-teacher status.
- *The professionals* would advocate better initial-teacher-training courses, closer links between these and schools as well as improved follow-up courses by means of INSET.

Cynics may suggest that the first half of the above political priority (ie, improving the supply of teachers at minimal cost) will remain unchanged during the 1990s even if there is a different political party in government. The Labour Party would not be troubled by a lunatic right-wing advocating laissez-faire, but the financial constraints will certainly continue to exist and encourage them to resist the pressure for massive all-round salary increases for teachers. One of the problems regarding teaching as a 'profession' is that there are simply too many teachers (nearly half a million) for them to be accorded elite status or to be paid professional salaries. Another Houghton-type across-the-board settlement will be unlikely.

I suggest that during the 1990s the major conflict will be between the need for greater professionalism and the inability (or unwillingness) to pay for an even larger and more expensive teaching force. A dramatic solution will be called for – namely a more hierarchical profession with a very different salary structure reflecting different levels of qualifications and training. But will any political party be prepared to take such a radical step?

Educational trends

Associated with the HMI concerns about professionalism referred to above are the educational developments related to teacher education. As far as decisions about official policies are concerned, it is probably fair to suggest that questions of educational theory are the least important! Yet there have been interesting developments in the last ten years which should not be ignored. There are also other educational developments of significance – not least the demands (and opportunities) presented to the teaching profession by the National Curriculum and its assessment.

Possibly the most significant development has been the change in thinking about educational theory and its relation to practice. Paul Hirst (1984) has, for example, referred to attempts made in the 1960s and 1970s to derive education theory from the disciplines of psychology, philosophy, sociology and history. He has shown how and why these attempts failed, and why it is now necessary to concentrate on generating educational theory out of good educational practice. Schön (1983) invented the term 'reflective practitioner' to sum up the relation between theory and practice in other practice-based professions as well as in education.

The implications of such changes for teacher education are in line with other aspects of professional development. Initial teacher training should be regarded as the first stage of initiation into the profession of teaching rather than a licence to practise for the next 40 years. Such training would then concentrate more on practical classroom skills and techniques and would not even pretend to provide a basis of philosophy, psychology or sociology for the rest of a professional lifetime. This would not mean, of course, that the traditional educational disciplines cease to possess any relevance – simply that they would perform a different function at a later professional stage. All this would reinforce some of the arguments of the James Report (Department of Education and Science, 1972) which suggested that initial teacher training should be followed by an induction period, and that later in their career all teachers should have the right to further professional study on a full-time basis.

Thus there will be good arguments in favour of a clear three-stage process of professional qualification: a variety of forms of initial training/licensing; followed by a period of probation/induction which would include further study before obtaining what is now referred to as qualified-teacher status; finally, after further very rigorous courses, full professional-teacher status would be gained with an appropriate advanced qualification in education – probably at Masters level (as is the practice in some states in the USA). Each of the three stages would be separated by real professional hurdles, and passing on to the next stage would be accompanied by a higher salary.

Such a phased approach to full professional qualification would help to reconcile some of the conflicts and contradictions described above. It should also be observed that the National Curriculum will, during the 1990s, be placing much greater responsibilities on teachers, not only in the organization and implementation of a highly structured curriculum, but also in its assessment. I suggest that the very demanding requirements of teacher assessment and standard assessment tasks should be the responsibility of professional teachers – not licensed teachers, probationers or those who have just reached qualified-teacher status which would thereby acquire a nice new meaning – (such teachers should only administer National Curriculum assessment and perform other professional duties if under the supervision and training of a fully professional teacher). The logic of this situation would be that all the Masters degrees in Education giving professional-teacher status would have to include appropriate courses covering the National Curriculum and its assessment.

A reasonable development of the 'CATE criteria' would be to propose a core curriculum for initial teacher training, specifying certain kinds of knowledge and skills that should be acquired by all beginning teachers. If this were to happen then the core curriculum idea might well be applied to those forms of INSET giving more advanced professional qualifications of the kind already described above.

Demographic trends

I suggested above that education developments were likely to have the least influence on government policies. Perhaps the most influential factors will be the demographic trends influencing, directly or indirectly, teacher supply and demand.

The first important fact to discuss is the clear rise in the school population during the 1990s: the figures for primary schools are, of course, known up to 1994–5, and can be projected for the rest of the decade. For secondary schools the base data are available, but choices such as the percentage of children staying on at school after age 16 cannot be predicted accurately. The trend for staying on is slightly upwards. An Institute of Manpower Studies study (Buchan and Weyman, 1989) projected an increase of over half a million primary pupils, between 1990 and 2000, plus 365,000 more pupils in secondary schools. Other things being equal – ie, assuming roughly the same pupil–teacher ratio – this would seem to indicate an increase in the demand for teachers of more than 40,000 by the end of the decade.

This fact would not in itself be unduly disturbing if it were not for other demographic factors operating at the same time. At least until 1996 there will be a fall in the number of school leavers, and a shortage of (or at least a greater demand for) graduates. In other words, there will be much greater competition for 'teacher material' than in previous years. This will provide a classic situation of increasing demand and diminishing supply which would – in a free market – lead to much higher salaries. But, of course, the market is not free. It is to some extent controlled by the DES (directly, by imposing 'quotas' on training institutions; indirectly, by policies on pupil–teacher ratios etc).

Several other factors in the supply–demand relationship complicate the formula, and will almost certainly aggravate the recruitment problem. One of the key characteristics of teacher supply is that it is heavily, and increasingly, dependent on females: in 1986–7, of the overall under-25 intake into teaching, only 21 per cent were male (32 per cent of secondary; only 9 per cent of primary (Buchan and Weyman, p 42). But during the 1990s other employers hungry for graduates will be trying to attract such young women into a variety of other graduate-level occupations where the salary structure and conditions of service may well be more attractive than teaching. (Over the years the attractiveness of teaching has tended to decline, whilst holidays and conditions of service on other 'comparable' occupations have improved.)

A further difficulty: in 1986–7, of the 14,500 female teachers recruited to primary schools, only about one-third were *new* entrants to the profession; approximately two-thirds were 're-entries' – women who had temporarily interrupted their career for child-rearing or other reasons. When questioned about teacher supply, DES politicians tend to make much of the fact that there are so many such trained teachers in the 'pool of inactive teachers' (PIT). But teachers in the 'PIT' are a rather unpredictable group, comparatively immobile, and open to other offers of employment – or no employment at all, if they so choose. Add to that the evidence provided by Professor Smithers (1989 and 1990) about the increasing rate of wastage in the profession, and we have a picture of teacher supply and retention during the 1990s which could become disastrous – unless appropriate action is taken. (Smithers's research indicates that teachers are leaving the profession at about five times the rate of official DES figures. This is a very important factor because in the past a key characteristic of the teaching force was its very low wastage rate: it seems extremely likely that this picture is changing.)

It may not just be difficult to recruit enough teachers during the 1990s – it may be impossible, if traditional routes are relied upon. Pressures to recruit more and more unqualified teachers or underqualified teachers will be enormous. The alternative may be to send children home from school untaught, or to resort to 'part-time schooling' – an outcome already predicted by the National Association of Schoolmasters and

Union of Women Teachers (NAS/UWT). Given such stark choices, it will be difficult for the teacher unions to resist pressures to employ the unqualified or underqualified. A better strategy for them might be to welcome such recruits as *assistants* for teachers and to concentrate on proper professional standards for those reaching full professional-teacher status. It would then be essential carefully to delineate the professional aspects of the teacher's role from the others.

Conclusion

All three trends – political, educational and demographic – seem to be taking teacher education in the same direction. Teaching is already a difficult and demanding job, and in the 1990s it will become more so, not least as a result of the National Curriculum and its assessment. The solution will be to have a more stratified teaching force where only the best qualified are regarded as professional teachers.

The role of the teacher will be changing considerably in any case. There is a good deal of research showing that, in spite of all the evidence, teachers still tend to spend too much time unproductively 'talking to' the whole class. Yet one of the fears expressed in connection with the National Curriculum is that teachers will have less time for just that kind of activity! During the 1990s there will certainly be changes in the nature of teaching, but it need not be to the detriment of the pupils. Teachers will spend more time assessing pupils, but they will also spend more time on curriculum planning – curriculum planning for individual pupils and small groups rather than the whole class. There will be less lecturing to the class as a whole. Teachers should not complain about that, but instead rejoice as experts in the management of learning and curriculum planning.

In the past when teachers talked about the individual differences of pupils, they tended to be thinking in one-dimensional terms about intelligence (and some teachers grouped children accordingly). But there is increasing evidence that intelligence is only one of many factors influencing how children learn. One of the tasks for professional teachers in the 1990s will be to diagnose other factors contributing to learning (or learning difficulty). Children certainly differ in terms of intelligence, but the IQ test is far too blunt an instrument as a diagnostic guide for improving learning. Some societies are far in advance of the UK in this respect.

For example, teachers in Ontario high schools have been urged to 'celebrate differences' in their students by becoming much more aware of the importance of 'learning styles' in the process of teaching and learning (Huff et al, 1986). The Ontario Secondary Schools Teachers

Federation (OSSTF) has given the project their full support and produced publications which popularize the available research in such fields as brain hemisphere specialization, gender differences in learning styles, imagery and learning, personality differences in learning, and so on. I have gained the impression from Canadian teachers that individual differences in learning are now being taken very seriously – not least in terms of professional development programmes – in Ontario and elsewhere in North America.

It may not be wildly optimistic to suggest that teacher education will flourish in the 1990s, but the process will be very different from the kind of courses which were common in the 1980s. Initial teacher education will tend to concentrate on shorter, more intensive courses, involving preparation for the classroom, perhaps deriving something from studies of the skills and competences required in the classrooms – without going to the extremes of some of the American competency-based courses. More of this training – but not all – will be school-based. There will still be a place for preparation for the next 40 years rather than the immediate requirements of survival in the classroom. During the second stage, induction/probation, the emphasis will change, encouraging teachers to reflect about their practice, as well as to become better practitioners. The third stage will concentrate on professional concerns: encouraging teachers to understand the curriculum as a whole, for example, and to reflect on teaching with reference, when appropriate, to the potential contributions of such disciplines as philosophy, psychology and sociology.

That will not be the end of the story. Professional teachers will need opportunities for continuous education, not only to update their 'subject expertise' and rethink their methods, but to develop as human beings and professionals in a variety of ways. Part-time research into the processes of teaching and learning should be a high priority for them. Only if measures such as these are taken will the young people of the 1990s get the quality teaching that they need and deserve.

References

Advisory Committee on the Supply and Education of Teachers (ACSET) (1983), 'Criteria and mechanisms for the approval of initial teacher training courses'. London: DES, 9 August.

Alexander, J L (1978), 'Collegiate teacher training in England and Wales: a study in the historical determinants of educational provision and practice in the mid-nineteenth century'. London: PhD thesis.

Alexander, R J, Craft, M and Lynch, J (eds) (1984), *Change in Teacher Education: context and provision since Robbins*. London: Holt, Rinehart and Winston.

Ashcroft, K and Griffiths, M (1989), 'Reflective teachers and reflective tutors: school experience in an initial teacher education course', *Journal of Education for Teaching* 15(1).

Ashton, P M E, Henderson, E S and Peacock, A (1989), *Teacher Education through Classroom Evaluation. The Principles and Practice of IT-INSET*. London: Routledge.

Balchin, R G A (1981), 'The quest for the General Teaching Council', *Education Today* 31 (3). Epping: College of Preceptors.

Barnett, C (1986), *Audit of War*. London: Macmillan.

Beattie, N (1985), *Professional Parents: Parent Participation in Four Western European Countries*. Lewes: Falmer Press.

Bell, A (1981), 'Structure, knowledge and social relationships in teacher education', *British Journal of Sociology in Education* 2(1).

Bernstein, B (1977), *Class, Codes and Control*. London: Routledge.

Bradbury, J L (1975), *Chester College and the Training of Teachers, 1839–1975*. Chester: Chester College.

Bruce, M G (1985), 'Teacher education since 1944: providing the teachers and controlling the providers', *British Journal of Educational Studies* 33(2), pp 164–72.

Buchan J and Weyman, C (1989), *The Supply of Teachers: A National Model for the 1990s*. Institute of Manpower Studies.

Burton, A (1977), 'Competency-based teacher education in the United States', *Compare* 7(1) pp 31–9.

Callahan, R E (1962), *Education and the Cult of Efficiency*. Chicago: University of Chicago Press.

Coldman, C (1989), 'Maths in a muddle', in: Deuchar (ed). (See below)

Conant, J (1963), *The Education of American Teachers*. New York: McGraw Hill.

Cox, C (1989), 'Unqualified approval', *Times Educational Supplement*, 6 January.

Cox, C, Marks, J, and Pomian-Srzednicki, M (1983), *Standards in English Schools*. London: National Council for Educational Standards, Report No 1.

Davies, H (1965), *Culture and the Grammar School*. London: Routledge.

Dawson, G (1981), 'Unfitting teachers to teach: sociology in the training of teachers', in a Flew et al, *The Pied Pipers of Education*. London: Social Affairs Unit.

Debenham, N (1989), 'First GCSE, now A level', in Deuchar (ed). (See below)

Dent, H C (1977), *The Training of Teachers in England and Wales, 1800–1975*. Sevenoaks: Hodder & Stoughton.

Department of Education and Science (1967), *Children and Their Primary Schools* (Plowden Report). London: HMSO.

Department of Education and Science (1968a), 'Inclusion of teachers on education committees', DES Press Notice, 19 August.

Department of Education and Science (1968b), 'Self-government for teachers', DES Press Notice, 4 October.

Department of Education and Science (1970), *A Teaching Council for England and Wales*, report of the working party appointed by the Secretary of State for Education and Science, Chairman T R Weaver. London: HMSO.

Department of Education and Science (1972), *Teacher Education and Training*, report of the James Committee. London: HMSO

Department of Education and Science (1978), *Primary Education in England*, a survey by HM Inspectors of Schools. London: HMSO

Department of Education and Science (1980), *PGCE in the Public Sector*, an HMI Discussion paper. London: DES.

Department of Education and Science (1981), *Teacher Training and the Secondary School*, an HMI discussion paper. London: DES.

Department of Education and Science (1983a), *Training in Schools: The Content of Initial Training*, HMI discussion paper. London: DES

Department of Education and Science (1983b), *Teaching Quality*, Cmnd 8836. London: HMSO.

Department of Education and Science (1984), *Initial Teacher Training: Approval of Courses*, Circular 3/84. London: DES.

Department of Education and Science (1987), *Quality in Schools: The Initial Training of Teachers*. London: HMSO.

Department of Education and Science (1988a), *Initial Teacher Training in Universities in England, Northern Ireland and Wales. A Review Carried out by HMI and the Inspectorate in Northern Ireland.* London: DES (Education Observed 7).

Department of Education and Science (1988b), *Secondary Schools: An Appraisal by HMI.* London: DES.

Department of Education and Science (1988c), *The New Teacher in School*, a survey by HM Inspectors in England and Wales, 1987. London: HMSO.

Department of Education and Science (1989a), *Standards in Education, 1987–1988: The Annual Report of HMI Senior Chief Inspector of Schools based on the Work of HMI in England.* London: DES.

Department of Education and Science (1989b), *Initial Teacher Training: Approval of Courses*, Circular 24/89. London: DES

Department of Education and Science (1989c), *Future Arrangements for the Accreditation of Courses of Inital Teacher Training: A Consultation Document.* London: DES.

Department of Education and Science (1989d), *Criteria for the Approval of Initial Teacher Training Courses.* London: DES.

Department of Education and Science (1990), *Standards in Education 1988–89: The Annual Report of HM Senior Chief Inspector of Schools*, London: DES.

Deuchar, S (ed) (1989), *What's Wrong with Our Schools?* London: Campaign for Real Education.

Dore, R (1976), *The Diploma Disease.* London: George Allen & Unwin.

Dow, G (1979), *Learning to Teach, Teaching to Learn*, London: Routledge.

Education Management Unit (1989), *Towards the General Teaching Council'.* EMU, 55 Gordon Square, London WC1H ONU.

Eisner, E W (1979), *The Educational Imagination.* New York: Macmillan.

Fish, D (1989), *Learning through Practice in Initial Teacher Training.* London: Kogan Page.

Furlong, V J, Hirst, P H, Pocklington, K, Miles, S (1988), *Initial Teacher Training and the Role of the School.* Milton Keynes and Philadelphia: Open University Press.

General Teaching Council for Scotland (1981), *Handbook* 4th edition. Edinburgh: General Teaching Council for Scotland.

Gordon, P (1986), 'Teaching as a graduate profession, 1890–1970', in J Wilkes (ed), *The Professional Teacher.* Leicester: History of Education Society pp 77–96.

Gosden, P H J H (1989), 'Teaching quality and the accreditation of initial teacher-training courses', in V A McClelland and V P Varma (eds), *Advances in Teacher Education.* London: Routledge, pp 1–18.

Handal, G and Lauri, P (1987), *Promoting Reflective Teaching – Supervision in Practice*. Milton Keynes: The Society for Research into Higher Education and Open University Press.

Hansard's *Parliamentary Debates* (1989), House of Lords 5 April 1989, *505*, no 60, columns 1162–82.

Hayek, F von (1988), *The Fatal Conceit* vol 1. London: Routledge.

Hillgate Group (1989), *Learning to Teach*. London: Claridge Press.

Hirst, P H (1984), 'Educational Theory', in P H Hirst (ed) *Educational Theory and its Foundation Disciplines*. London: Routledge.

Hirst, P H (1985), 'Educational studies and the PGCE course', *British Journal of Educational Studies* 33(3), pp 211–21.

Hoyle, E (1980), 'Professionalization and deprofessionalization in education', in E Hoyle and J Megarry (eds), *Professional Development of Teachers: World Yearbook of Education 1980*. London: Kogan Page, pp. (42–54).

Huff, P et al (1986), *Teaching and Learning Styles*. Ontario: Ontario Secondary School Teachers Foundation.

Jackson J A (1970), *Professions and Professionalization*. Cambridge: Cambridge University Press.

Jones, L G E (1924), *The Training of Teachers in England and Wales: A Critical Survey*. Oxford: Oxford University Press.

Judge, H G (1988), 'Cross-national perceptions of teachers', *Comparative Education Review* 32(2), pp 143–58.

Kay-Shuttleworth, J P (1862), *Four Periods of Public Education*. London: Longman.

Kirk, G (1985), *Teacher Education and Professional Development*. Edinburgh: Scottish Academic Press.

Koerner, J (1963), *The Miseducation of American Teachers*. Boston: Houghton Mifflin.

Labour Party (1989), *Children First: Labour's Policy for Raising Standards in Schools*. London: The Labour Party.

Larson, M S (1977), *The Rise of Professionalism: A Sociological Analysis*. Berkeley: University of California Press.

Lauglo, J (1982), 'Rural primary school teachers as potential community leaders? Contrasting historical cases in Western countries', *Comparative Education* 18(3), pp 233–55.

Lawton, D (1984), *The Tightening Grip*, Bedford Way Papers. London: Institute of Education, University of London.

Lawton, D (1989), *Education, Culture and the National Curriculum*. London: Hodder & Stoughton.

Lieberman, M (1956), *Education as a profession*. New York: Prentice Hall.

Lomax, D E (ed) (1973), *The Education of Teachers in Britain*. London: John Wiley.

Lucas, P (1988), 'An approach to research based teacher education through collaborative enquiry', *Journal of Education for Teaching* 14(1).

Lynn, R (1988), *Educational Achievements in Japan: Lessons for the West.* London: Social Affairs Unit.

McNamara, J and O'Keeffe, D (1988), 'Roots of madness', *Encounter*, September.

McNee, M (1989), 'The nonsense these academics come up with', in Deuchar (ed). (See above)

Magoon, A J (1976), 'Teaching and performance-based teacher education', in Lomax (ed) pp 235–62.

Mallinson, V (1980), *The Western European Idea in Education.* London: Pergamon Press.

Mannheim, K (1954), *Ideology and Utopia.* London: Routledge.

Miller, J (1981), 'The General Teaching Council for Scotland', *Education Today* 31 (3). Epping: College of Preceptors.

Musgrove, F (1978), 'Curriculum, culture and ideology', *Journal of Curriculum Studies* 10(2).

Newcastle Commission Report (1861), P.P. XXl.i.

O'Hear, A (1988), *Who Teaches the Teachers?* London: Social Affairs Unit.

O'Keeffe, D (1985), 'Swann-song of prejudice', *Encounter*, November.

O'Keeffe, D (ed) (1986), *The Wayward Curriculum.* London: Social Affairs Unit.

Orwell, G (1970), *Collected Essays, Journalism and Letters* vol 2, p 168; vol 3, 142. Harmondsworth: Penguin.

Palmer, F (1986), 'Reducing English to short-cut skills', in: O'Keeffe (ed). (See above)

Partington, G (1986), 'History, rewritten in ideological fashion', in: O'Keeffe (ed). (See above)

Patrick, H (1986), 'From Cross to CATE: the universities and teacher education over the past century', *Oxford Review of Education* 12(3).

Popper, K (1972), *Objective Knowledge.* Oxford: Clarendon Press.

Prais, S J and Wagner, K (1985), 'Schooling standards in England and Germany: some comparisons bearing on economic performance', *National Institute Economic Review*, May.

Raison, T (1966), 'In defence of the professions', *New Society*, 18 August.

Ree, H A (1956), *The Essential Grammar School.* London: George Harrap.

Rich, R W (1933, 1972), *The Training of Teachers in England and Wales during the Nineteenth Century.* Cambridge: Cambridge University Press; Bath: Cedric Chivers.

Schön, D A (1971), *Beyond the Stable State.* London: Temple Smith.

Schön, D A (1983), *The Reflective Practitioner.* London: Temple Smith.

Schön, D A (1987), *Educating the Reflective Practitioner.* San Francisco/ London: Jossey-Bass.

Scruton, R (1985), *World Studies – Education or Indoctrination?* London: Institute for European Defence and Strategic Studies.

Segalman, R and Marsland, D (1989), *Cradle to Grave.* London: Macmillan and the Social Affairs Unit.

Sexton, S (ed) (1988), *GCSE: A Critical Analysis.* Warlingham, Surrey: IEA Education Unit.

Simon, B (1981), 'Why no pedagogy in England?', in B Simon and W Taylor (eds), *Education in the Eighties: The Central Issues.* London: Batsford Academic & Educational, pp 124–45.

Smithers, A and Robinson, P (1989), 'Loss from Teaching'. Manchester: University of Manchester.

Smithers, A (1990), 'Teacher Loss', interim report to Leverhulme Trust. Manchester: University of Manchester.

Smyth, J (ed) (1987), *Educating Teachers: Changing the Nature of Pedagogical Knowledge.* Lewes: Falmer Press.

Soloman, J (1987), 'New thoughts on teacher education', *Oxford Review of Education* 13(3).

Stenhouse, L (1987), *An Introduction to Curriculum Research and Development.* London: Heinemann.

Stevens, F (1960), *The Living Tradition: The Social and Educational Assumptions of the Grammar School.* London: Hutchinson.

Stones, E (1978), 'Psychopedagogy: theory and practice in teaching', *British Educational Research Journal* 4(2).

Stones, E (1984), *Supervision in Teacher Education.* London: Methuen.

Sutherland, M (1985), 'The Place of Theory of Education in Teacher Education', *British Journal of Educational Studies* 33(3), pp 222–34.

Swanwick, K (1989), *Teacher Education and the PGCE: A Research Report.* London: Institute of Education, University of London.

Swift, D (1972), 'What is the environment?', in K Richardson and D Spears (eds), *Race, Culture and Intelligence.* Harmondsworth: Penguin.

Taylor, W (1984), 'The National Context, 1972–1982', in Alexander, Craft and Lynch (eds), pp 16–30. (See above)

Thomasson, R (1969), 'Home rule for teachers?' *New Society,* 25 September.

Tibble, J M (1966), *The Study of Education.* London: Routledge.

Tickle, L (1987), *Learning Teaching, Teaching Teaching: A Study in Partnership in Teacher Education.* Lewes: Falmer.

Tuck, J (1973a), 'From day training college to university department of education', in Lomax (ed), pp 71–94.

Tuck, J (1973b), 'The university departments of education: their work and their future', in Lomax (ed) pp 95–116. (See above)

Tyack, D (1974), *The One Best System: A History of American Urban Education*. Cambridge: Harvard University Press.

Waller, W (1965), *The Sociology of Teaching*. New York: John Wiley & Sons.

Weber, M (1948), *Max Weber, Essays in Sociology*, translated and edited by H H Gerth and C W Mills. London: Routledge.

Wiles, P J D, (1977), *Economic Institutions Compared*. Oxford: Blackwell.

Willey, E T and Maddison, R E (1971), *An Enquiry into Teacher Training*. London: University of London Press.

Wilson, J (1975), *Educational Theory and the Preparation of Teachers*. Windsor: NFER.

Wragg, E C (1974), *Teaching Teaching*. Newton Abbot: David and Charles.

Wragg, E C (1984), 'The classroom in focus', *Times Educational Supplement*, 24 February.

Wragg, E C (ed) (1984), *Classroom Teaching Skills*. Beckenham: Croom Helm.

Zeichner, K M (1981), 'Reflective teaching and field-based experience in teacher education', *Interchange* 12, pp 1–22.

Zeichner, K M and Listor, D P (1982), 'Teaching students to reflect', *Harvard Educational Review* 57, pp 23–48.

Index